TREASURED STORIES

INSPIRED BY THE

HOLY SPIRIT

"From now on the Advocate, the Holy Spirit whom the Father will send in my name, will teach you all things and remind you of all that I told you."
(John 14:26)

INSPIRATIONAL STORIES

compiled with reflections

LANNI FIDES

Tellwell Talent
www.tellwell.ca

ISBN
978-0-2288-8507-8 (Hardcover)
978-0-2288-8506-1 (Paperback)
978-0-2288-8508-5 (eBook)

TABLE OF CONTENTS

DEDICATION

To

my loving husband, Stephen
our beloved children and families:

Jasmine & husband Jeremiah, children Jean & Jermaine
Matthew & wife Raelyn, children Raphael & Mae Lily
& husband Marty, children Christopher & Maya

my loving sister Jade
all relatives and friends

and

You, my readers

Acknowledgements

Deepest gratitude for the motivation,
inspiration and support of:

my loving family

Catholic Church Parish of St. John 23rd Stanhope
Gardens and its Ministries of the Word and
Special Religious Education, NSW, Australia

Community of Couples for Christ
Australia and its Ministries

My Chapter-Seniors' Household, NSW, Australia

To all the Brothers and Sisters who willingly shared
their life journey inspired by the Holy Spirit

and

Society of St Paul, NSW Australia

Introduction

It was a wintry cold night, right after my night prayers, when all of a sudden, I felt the blow of warm air on my face which instantaneously prodded me of the breath of the Holy Spirit! I asked GOD, "Oh Lord God, what is your message for me?"

An inspirational story shared by a sister, was stuck in my mind for almost a week!

I was seated comfortably in a medical clinic waiting for my name to be called by the medical receptionist, but a bit disappointed when I turned around and saw a long queue. Then, a middle-aged lady, with sad eyes sat next to me, and started a friendly chat. I saw tears in her eyes, but felt the peace and joy in her heart. I became curious and politely asked her, if she was okay. And unexpectedly, she started to narrate what just happened to her five months ago. I was completely immersed into her story; I can visualise all the events she told me in details, like a movie in my mind. I was amazed by her boldness and made me wonder why I was chosen to be the blessed listener to this very inspirational life journey!

From that very day I had met this amazing woman of faith and shared with me her heart-warming life story, every night, during my prayers I kept on asking God's message through the Holy Spirit, what He wanted me to do! I mysteriously felt that I have to do something, but couldn't identify what it was! I fervently prayed for the Holy Spirit's intervention. Finally, I felt that God wants me to put into writing this extraordinary story and some beautiful stories of people which were truly inspired by the Holy Spirit! I slept so peacefully after that clear message and even dreamed of the lists of things to do in this divine mission given to me.

So, this motivational book came into conception once I'd received affirmations and signs to start this divine mission of proclaiming God's unconditional love and faithfulness to His people. These inspirational stories will serve as instruments in influencing people's lives upon reading them and may discover lessons from them which are useful tools in facing their day-to-day challenges.

I had started to think of my friends and relatives whom I knew had lived a very inspiring and meaningful life journey, for I, myself got motivated and inspired by their remarkable experiences. All the projected plans went on 'smooth sailing' and I was overwhelmed with joy when twenty-two exceptional and inspirational stories of people filled up my journal, which I can profoundly note and trumpet as ***"Treasured Stories Inspired by the Holy Spirit."***

After almost four months of constant communications with the sisters and brothers, who unselfishly and willingly said "Yes" to the Lord to be instruments to inspire other people through their notable life stories and of course, most importantly through God's blessings and graces, this inspirational book came into fruition!

Each story is followed by my short personal reflections giving some insights, awareness and affirmations about the remarkable life journey.

Do you want to know these amazing stories? Why were they noted as "Treasured Stories inspired by the Holy Spirit?

Well, it's time to relax and read over a cup of tea or coffee! Enjoy and be inspired!

Lanni Fides
September 29, 2022

My Three Children are Angels in Heaven

"Make the Lord your delight, and He will grant your heart's desire. Commit your way to the Lord; put your trust in Him and let Him act."

(Psalm 37: 4-5)

In the bush of far north of West Australia, there lived a big family where in each member was designated with a specific job or employment in order to meet the everyday needs and essentials. As a norm, the women were in charge of household chores; men were the bread winners and out before the early morning sunrise to earn their daily wages. These men worked for the railways under the scorching heat of the sun during summer and icy blast cold weather during winter. Such was a hard and arduous manual labour during those olden days!

Marla, in her early twenties, was the oldest among the children whose job was to cook for the family and her father's team of men working in the area. It was a struggle for Marla as this job demands an early morning wake-up and late sleep, preparing and cooking for the hard-working men as well as her own family.

Marla's life had changed dramatically, when one day her uncle came to visit and took her to a regional farm in New South Wales as a housemaid for a farming family, with the approval of her parents. After some years on the farm, Marla discovered that she was pregnant. She was totally confused and decided to write home and inform her parents about her condition. Her boyfriend shockingly just abandoned her and said he wasn't ready for a family! To make this situation worst was when she received the saddest and shocking reply from her parents firmly stating, "You can come home, or the baby, but not both." She felt like heavens fell on her head and cried bitterly!

What was she to do? She would have to work. She could have an abortion and that would have made it a lot easier, or would it? In the midst of pains and struggles as you could imagine, Marla decided and managed to keep the baby. Until that special day when a tiny and frail baby girl was born into this mysterious world and named her Marita. This was how I came into being!

My mother found it impossible to work and at the same time keep me on her own, so sadly, she put me up for adoption. Anna, my adoptive mother gave me all the care and love likened to a real mother. I remembered all my life how Anna kept on telling me stories about my real mother, her own hardest blow in life to leave me in order to keep me alive, but delighted to know that her baby will surely be loved and looked after. Heaven blessed me with a very loving mother in the person of Anna. She tirelessly kept reminding me to search for my real mother, for she knew that one day she would not be around to look after me. At significant events in my life, like my confirmation, engagement, as well as after my wedding day, I sought for my mother upon Anna's suggestions.

Persistence, perseverance and determination won with the triumph of locating my mother, but devastated to know that Marla, my real mother had already passed away. This later on led me to meet my old grandparents and my family heritage. They all warmly welcomed me and my poor old grandparents asked for my forgiveness in rejecting me during that dark period of my mother's life. I felt their remorse and sincere heart-breaking emotions of guilt which made me cried bitterly also releasing my pain of resentments towards them and led us all to hug and embrace each other and humbly uttered all my words of love and forgiveness, combined with the sounds of sobs and sniffles from everyone. It was indeed a very dramatic scene like that of a drama series in the television! I completely felt joy and peace in my heart! Thank You, Oh Lord!

Recollecting all the hardships I'd encountered like a lost sheep in the wilderness, I felt the great consolation of knowing that there is God up in the sky watching over me and keeping me safe. There were several times when I stepped on dangerous soil and He protected me. With full trust and faith in God, I moved on in my journey with an expectant faith of hope for a better future with my loving husband. We'd settled in the northern region of New South Wales with an average earning capacity of Paulo enough for a family with six children. Yes, there was the great joy and contentment in the family, as we just led a very simple life on the farm where everything was almost available and free as long as we kept on digging the soil and endlessly planting seeds for crops and vegetables perfect for everyday consumption. We also had few chickens and ducks around the backyard for eggs and meat especially during winter season. But God tested our hearts, how strong we could be in this pain and anxiety which we'd endured day in and day out.

You see, we had these three older children, Lucille, Anne and Patrick who were all shockingly diagnosed with cystic fibrosis during their infancy stage. It is a disorder that damages the lungs and digestive system. Paulo and I were absolutely devastated when we learned from the doctor that this is a life-threatening disease and the children could suffer pains which lead to death at any given age or time. We fervently prayed to God to spare the children and just lived each day at a time with full surrender to His will. It was at this point that I told my husband not to try for any more babies, but if it was God's will for us to have more, then we would gladly accept His will. I totally handed over myself to GOD!

I fell pregnant and gave birth to a healthy baby girl and named her Mirla. The very first check-up of the baby gave us the greatest news that she was FREE from the disease! Praise God! She grew up as a normal and healthy baby. Then after two years, God blessed us with another baby girl Lilia and was FREE from the disease as well. Just after a year, a baby boy was born whom we named Amos. I'd witnessed Paulo's over joyous emotion, as he had been waiting for a male child, someone to be the next in line in the management of the farm! Again, praise God! he was FREE from the disease! We were all in jubilation to hear this wonderful news. So, immediately we had organised a Thanksgiving Mass in our local church followed by fellowship at home. It was indeed, a solemn and delightful celebration!

"After joy comes sorrow," as the saying goes. Paulo and I had started to feel our pain and agony in witnessing the severe sufferings of the first three older children diagnosed with cystic fibrosis dying one by one. Lucille died at the age of fifteen, Anne at the age of sixteen and Patrick at twenty-five years old! Each time a child dies, I felt the sword pierced deeply in my heart! Such an excruciating pain which led me to think of the Blessed Mother Mary's presence during the agony of her son Jesus dying on the cross! My pain was absolutely incomparable to her anguish and afflictions! Help me Oh Lord God Jesus to be strong like Your Mother!

My greatest joy and comfort with full faith is knowing that these three blessed children are all in Heaven with all the angels and saints, as "Three Angels" too! We'd prepared them spiritually to be ready to face God anytime, as death sneaks in like a thief in the night. Their health situation was not a secret in the family, so the younger children understood very well that their older sisters and older brother, one day will be gone to Heaven. We'd also explained to them what Heaven is, a beautiful place like paradise, where the Heavenly God the Father dwells in eternity!

I'd realised, all through the years that my walk had been a walk of total surrender to God's will and this had given me these sweet fruits of love, peace, joy, forgiveness and endless gratitude which forever will dwell in my heart! My God is very alive to me! Without Him, I am nothing. I take Him everywhere I go. I know that He is always beside me, guiding me and showing me signs all the time. Thank You, Oh Lord! Praise and Glory to You, Oh God Almighty!

Reflections

Indeed! what an inspirational story! Marita's life story was absolutely inspired by the Holy Spirit. Her life journey had clearly manifested the presence of God's divine providence and certainly, the guidance of the Holy Spirit! Why is that? It is because Marita is a woman of faith! Knowing that she was only an adopted child, had made her attachment and connection with God stronger. She had chosen the right way to cling more and seek God's help and love and hence, had developed this deep and close relationship with Jesus and His Mother, the Blessed Mother Mary. She never lost hope in searching for her real mother and ancestry in order to find her true identity. True enough, through her virtues of persistence and perseverance, she victoriously found her ancestry, though sadly her real mother had already passed away. All through the years, she had totally relied on God's holy presence and guidance in her day-to-day journey. In the absence of her real mother, she found comfort and company with God and the Blessed Mother Mary!

As she had mentioned, "My walk had been a walk of total surrender to God's will!" I personally love this quotation! I firmly believe that by following this kind of life pattern of total and full surrender to God's will, each and every one of us would never be lost into the darkness of the wilderness, but rather would be led to the bright path of a beautiful life!

"It is those who walk in the Spirit of
God who are children of God."
(Romans 8:14)

STORY 2

I Married a Caucasian Man!

"I still have many things to tell you, but you cannot bear them now. When he, the Spirit of truth comes, he will guide you into all the truth. He will not give his own message, but will speak only of what he hears, and he will declare to you the things to come."
(John 16: 12-13)

I am Pia, born of an average income family of ten children. Of the four girls, I am the only one with chestnut brownish skin colour and my other three sisters have fair skin. Since childhood, my siblings had always teased me as an adopted child because of my colour. I just took it as a joke, but deep inside me I was in pain, hurt and embarrassed. I used to go inside my room and cry holding my favourite doll with long hair, beautiful eyes and pretty dress; knell down in front of a picture of Jesus and complain to him, telling him of my siblings' meanness and naughtiness. After my burst of emotions, I felt peace and calmness in my heart, especially when our loving mother follows me to my room, comforts and hugs me saying, "Don't listen to them and just ignore them. I already gave them what they deserved."

When I turned into a teenager, my dream was to marry a foreigner. In my country, a foreigner is always considered a Caucasian with light coloured skin person. You can imagine why? You may say that this is vanity! I was just thinking of my future children! I don't want them to have my colour and protect them from the mockery and harsh jokes of people! I prayed to God to listen to my plea!

I studied diligently in college, until I finished my Education Degree with flying colours and proudly started my noble career as an elementary school teacher in a nearby town. All of my three sisters got married early and unfortunately weren't able to finish their college degrees to the disappointment of our parents. All of them have their own respective families with three children each, while I got so busy with my studies and forgot to fall in love. I just concentrated on my career in teaching children which is my first love!

Until one day, out of the blue, I received a letter from an Irish man named James! How on earth did this foreigner know my name and address? Is this God's answer to my prayer? I couldn't understand my emotions at that time! You may think that I must be happy and excited to meet this foreigner, right? I was, but anxious because I had no idea, how he had known my details! I became so curious to unfold this mystery!

Later on in our correspondence, James honestly admitted that I wasn't even the girl he intended to send a letter. He lost the piece of paper where the name and address of the original girl was written, and miraculously somebody gave my details! So, my ego was a bit stung, being a second choice, but I quickly consoled myself saying, "This must be your mysterious ways Oh Lord God Almighty!"

After two months, James flew in to my country to personally meet me! At the airport, straight away he said, "Oh I like very much your brownish tan colour!" Surprised and quite embarrassed I answered him back and said, "Oh! thank you and I adore your colour too!" We both laughed loud and long enough for others to look at us and wonder what's going on? And believe it or not we fell in love at each other at first sight! God is good!

Since he flew back into his country, I regularly received his letters mainly updating me of the status of my application for migration as his fiancée. Time flew fast, and true to his words, I arrived in Ireland the following year. My three sisters were all so envious of my fate and all cried when they sent me off at the airport and most of all asked for my forgiveness for being so mean to me since we were little girls. I cried out my hidden resentments towards them and hugged them all, while uttering my words of forgiveness. I felt the most peaceful and joyful emotions at that very moment, until we all said our sad, but sweet goodbyes with hugs and kisses!

James and I tied our knots in the Sacrament of Matrimony in our local Catholic Church, through the kindness and generosity of our parish priest. A simple and solemn wedding was celebrated through the Holy Mass followed by the Matrimonial Rites, attended by James' parents, few relatives and close friends. With James' casual job, money was a big issue to us at that time, so with our beloved parish priest's support, everything was made possible which forever we will be grateful! To add excitement to my story, James had won a certain amount of money from betting games and this money paid off our reception bills! I know it's not right because the money came from gambling, but I do believe that God understands us, for He is an ever-loving, generous and merciful GOD!

Time is ticking away, and James truly long for children, as he was getting older. We hoped and prayed that very soon I would fall pregnant. After two years, we decided to see a fertility specialist, with specialised training in gynaecology and obstetrics. After several tests performed, James and I were so devastated when the specialist said that I had endometriosis which meant I can't have kids! As if, I felt the sky fell on my head and uttered these words, "Lord God Almighty, help me! I beg You Lord, even only one child, Lord God, help me, have mercy on me!"

With downtrodden spirits, we passed by the local church where we got married and cried out our disappointment and in silence, we just let tears cleansed our heavy burden. On our way out, the parish priest saw us and greeted us briefly. He noticed our sadness, so we told him what happened. He, then suggested to get another opinion. "Oh, that's a great idea! Thank you, Father!" I felt so hopeful with that suggestion and with full expectant faith, something good and bright is coming ahead of us!

We went to see another doctor and he explained very well what this endometriosis is all about. He said that it is a disorder in which tissue that normally lines the uterus grows outside it. The displaced tissue may cause internal inflammations which leads to pain and sometimes infertility in many women. I had succumbed to all his medical advice and treatment as well as surrendered to God our fervent prayers and plea for a child.

After a year of treatment, the biggest blessing in our life was granted! I got pregnant and God blessed us with a beautiful baby girl and christened her Marie Kirsten! Thank You, Oh Lord! Praise God Almighty!

The period of raising Marie Kirsten was a delight, being a quiet and healthy baby. It was now my husband whom I missed so much because he was always away for party events and functions, being an entertainer, singer and dancer. I can't see him anymore during weekends. I was busy looking after our baby and he was busy with his own business.

I clearly remembered the words that my mother used to tell me. "Life is not always a bed of roses, but, also some thorns!" My husband turned out to be a drunkard, alcoholic and a gambler too! He encountered so many troubles with the police. To make it worst, I heard of some rumours going around our little neighbourhood that he was involved with flings and love affairs with other women. With my heart broken, I can't carry it anymore, so I packed up our bags, together with our baby, and left him! I faithfully prayed for him and never stopped hoping for I know one day he will be awakened from this darkness of sin. This passage from Luke 1:31 "With God nothing is impossible!" had kept me hopeful and going in my day-to-day challenges.

One night, James rang me and begged us to come home with a threat that he will kill himself if we continue being away from him! He sounded like drunk, so at first, I just ignored him. But later on, I thought of a possibility that he might really do it. So quickly I left the baby to my in-laws and hastily took off to our house and found James, snoring soundly asleep. "Thank You Lord! If not, I will be guilty all my life in abandoning him, instead of helping him out of his bad habits!"

Years went by, James and I still had occasional dramas, but with the power of the Holy Spirit, I maintained my calmest, coolest and peaceful spirit. With the support and prayers of my prayer group run by the charismatic community in our Church, I became firmer and stronger in my faith ready to face heavy challenges. All my pains were all compensated with our God's miracle baby Kirsten's excellent performance in her studies. From her high school days up to her journey to the prestigious university in the city, she had been a recipient of the highest awards and granted government subsidy for her university expenses. What a great blessing and graces from the Lord!

While our daughter was in the city, I felt so lonely as James still continued his weekend commitments. He was unstoppable, because of his passion for music and art! How I wish that we could be together on Sundays to attend the mass, pray and serve together in our church and community! So, I just accepted his passion because this made him happy. I sacrificed my own little happiness and spent more time with my prayer group and serve in our church. I patiently prayed for James to have a change of heart and begged God to touch and enlighten him and one day join me in my prayers in order to have faith and trust in the Lord as well.

Until one night, James had a seizure and I hurriedly called an ambulance. He stayed for few days in the hospital waiting for results from his several tests. Later on, the doctor gave the announcement that James was diagnosed with epilepsy! He was not allowed to go in crowded places as this will trigger his condition! Oh Lord, my God! You always work in mysterious ways!

True enough, as days, weeks and months had passed, I continuously and patiently prayed for James to join me in my faith. After a year, I received the biggest surprise in my life! He said to me one night, "Pia, my sweetest, ever-loving and patient wife, I will join you in your prayers!" I nearly stumbled upon hearing those sweetest words, so I fell on my knees and PRAISE and THANK GOD! I cried tears of JOY and VICTORY! My husband, once asleep and lived in darkness has now been awakened into the LIGHT OF CHRIST! PRAISE GOD ALMIGHTY!

Reflections

WOW! What a great model of an ever faithful and loving wife! True and faithful to her marriage vow of: "In the name of God, I take you James, to be my husband, to have and to hold you from this day forward, for better, for worse, for richer, for poorer, in sickness and in health, to love and to cherish, till death do us part."

Pia's patience, peaceful spirit and joyful soul are truly from the fruits of the Holy Spirit! Being a very prayerful woman from a little girl, hidden from the cocoon of shyness and bitterness due to her colour, eventually evolved her into a beautiful, shining and colourful butterfly! Being a woman of strong faith, most of all, turned her into a powerful woman of God! Her virtues of humility and an ever-forgiving heart, were all shown from her persona based from her remarkable story. She had performed her duty as a loving mother to her only daughter Marie Kirsten; as faithful and patient wife to James, no matter how his erroneous ways had tremendously hurt her, still stood strong, firm and steadfast with full hope and faith to her eternal and loving God! Praise to You, Oh Lord God Almighty!

> *"Happy the man who trusts in the Lord, and whose confidence is in him! He is like a tree planted near water, that thrusts its roots towards the stream. It has no fear when the heat comes, its leaves are always green; in the year of drought, it has no worries and it always bears fruit."*
> *(Jeremiah 17:7-8)*

My Trauma on "Social Media"

"I sought the Lord, and he answered me; from all my fears, he delivered me. Those who look to him are radiant with joy, their faces are never clouded with shame. Oh, taste and see that the Lord is good! Blessed is the one who finds shelter in him!"
(Psalm 34: 4-5, 8)

"From now on, we don't have a daughter named Jovy!" These were the words from my mother that kept on ringing in my ears all through the years!

I grew up to be a troubled child until I'd reached my teenage life, which is often called as the most challenging and difficult stage in a man's life due to many changes happening in the body, like physically, emotionally, mentally and socially. I fell into the trap of a puppy love. I thought I truly love my classmate Pete because I found comfort and joy when I was with him.

Mistakenly, I got into an uncontrolled involvement sexually and devastatingly fell pregnant.

When I've learned about my pregnancy, I didn't know what to do. I had no choice but to be brave and face the music and so I told my parents about my situation. And that was the time when my mother uttered those words of disownment! I sadly left home with bitter tears of guilt and regret and told my boyfriend Pete. We were so young and still on illegal age to get married. So, I lived with Pete and his family, until I gave birth to a baby boy and named him Jay. Both Pete and I stopped studying high school and concentrated on earning money to help us in our everyday needs. After two years, we had our second baby boy whom we named Joel. They both grew up so healthy with God's divine providence. Pete found a better paying job and things were getting better in our family, until a tragic accident happened. Joel was missing for few days and found dead near the river! He got drowned when the strong-fast current abruptly came and he was taken. Everything had changed from then on. With my heart broken due to the tragic loss of poor Joel, added pain and anguish when Pete started to be violent and abusive towards me and Jay. It was an unbearable pain, so, I took Jay with me and left him. With my little savings, we managed to go to the city and started our new life.

Since I was disowned by my parents, I turned to God and His Beloved Mother Mary; regularly prayed to Jesus and asked for the help and intercession from His Blessed Mother. As we travelled towards the city, Jay and I prayed the rosary. Then the lady seated next to us heard our prayers and curiously asked where we're heading to! With tears in my eyes, I boldly told her our story. Like an angel sent from heaven, she generously offered us to stay temporarily at her house, until I find a job!

Jay grew up to be a good and responsible young man. He performed very well in his studies in high school. Claire, our landlady was so impressed with him too. When I found the job, we paid her rent and she only charged us with the lowest rental fee! She even advised me to continue my studies because I was still young at that time. So, I did! I finished my last year of high school and enrolled straight at the nearest college, studying at night. Both Jay and myself excelled in our classes and happily gave updates to Claire, as if she was my mother and Jay's grandmother! God is really good!

In college, I met Luis who also excelled in his studies and a popular guy among girls in the campus, due to his charm of being a funny and a smart guy. He started to show affection and some interest in me through his constant gifts of flowers and chocolates. Once again, my heart started to beat and I fell in love with him. This time, we got married properly in church and had three children, Jodie, Josh and Joseph. Sadly, Joseph, the youngest died when he was a baby, born with a weak heart. This loss of a baby had opened once again, my trauma on the death of poor Joel. I cried out my pain and anguish to the Lord with my non-stop wailing and crying, until I felt no more tears from my eyes. Luis hugged and comforted me and we both prayed together.

There was an open family migration to Canada sometime in the middle of 1980s, and Luis grabbed that opportunity. Together with our three children- Jay, Jodie, and Josh, we successfully passed all the requirements and started a new life in our newly found home!

With our educational qualifications, Luis and I both landed into really good paying jobs, more than enough to sustain and maintain our daily needs and send the three children to good schools. We lived a stable and comfortable lives and not neglected our spiritual needs. Sundays to us meant going to mass and spend quality time together. We also joined a Catholic charismatic community for our teenage children to mingle with and build friendship with teenagers of the same faith. As parents, we found the value of being together with a group of families and their children with the same moral values to avoid derailments as based from my personal experience. I truly became so protective over my children, especially with Jodie. All of the children were all doing well in their studies and nearly finishing their high school and college education. I was so happy and contented with our family life style and couldn't ask for anything more! God abundantly blessed us with our own dream house and comfortable living, with sufficient income enough to sustain all our finances and miscellaneous expenses.

In the early 2000, the rise of social media began, which had changed the world! The fast, rapid and vast acceptance of these technologies had changed the ways how people find partners through dating sites, how people accessed daily news and how people can demand political changes. So many social media platforms started to sprout like mushrooms; to mention a few: Myspace, Facebook, WhatsApp, and Twitter. People's means of communication revolted like a big bang on mobile phones of different brands with all sorts of modern accessories, as well as PCs and laptops. I was totally overwhelmed with the rapid digitalised world through unending innovations on modern technologies.

This dramatically had changed our family's daily routine and grievously affected our relationship as a couple. It slowly affected our family relationship especially with communications. Our children had their own mobile phones and computers. And also, Luis had purchased his own mobile and laptop! He believed that his children must not be left behind with technology, but rather be ahead! Honestly, I wasn't happy at all with what was happening in our family! We hardly talked to each other. After dinner, everyone goes to his/her own room with mobiles and computers on, to check on emails and messages. We seemed to be strangers in our own homes and not a family anymore! This was insane and our children were unstoppable because their father was exactly and fanatically on the same page with them!

I kept my peace and just let everyday passed by without a word to avoid arguments, but I was uncomfortable and unhappy with the sudden changes in our household. Our newly built house of four bedrooms, and one study room was big enough to have everyone settled comfortably in their own world of mobile phones and computers. And where was I? Of course, in the kitchen, my peaceful and quiet corner!

One night, I noticed that Luis locked himself in the study room and stayed there for several hours. It was past midnight and he was still there. I got worried that something might had happened to him, so I knocked at the door and he was still awake! His excuse was that he had to fix a big issue at work and must submit his report in the morning. I naively accepted that and went back to sleep. But this was an everyday occurrence and to me, it already looked suspicious! So, I've started to ask him questions and to my surprise he got upset and yelled at me at the top of his voice! I saw him as a different person, and accused me of not understanding him, while he was doing everything for our family's sake! Oh, his behaviour had totally shocked me and just left the room and cried out to God and to the Blessed Mother Mary!

On a Monday morning, right after breakfast, as usual, was the rush hours of going towards everyone's destinations that is school and work. But Luis stayed and said that he was still finalising an important financial report to be submitted to his boss and will leave soon. So, he was left alone at the house. With the presence of my innate intuition as a woman, I deeply felt that something was really wrong with Luis, so I fervently prayed for him and intensely surrendered him to God for guidance! I just felt so worried and anxious about his recent unusual behaviour. Oh, God please help me to have a peaceful heart!

It was nine o'clock at night and Luis wasn't home yet! At this time of the night, everyone in our household had already settled down from shower to dinner and had relaxed a bit before bed. Until all the children were all in their respective rooms at ten o'clock and Luis was still missing. I hastily called his mobile and shockingly was switched off! It was past midnight, when I decided to call his boss and ask about Luis, thinking that he might be with him for emergency meetings. I was devastated when he told me that he had filed his one-month annual leave two weeks ago and commenced today! My troubled heart kept me awake the whole night and can't wait for the morning to come, so I can start ringing around his workmates and friends whom I thought were close to him and might know something about his personal issues. All of them were also shocked and unfortunately had no idea at all about his personal plans. One of the close friends suggested that I must report him as "a missing person" immediately and which I did! That very day, the police force had started the search and executed its communication network strategies which had continued for a week. For the meantime, our own family together with our relatives, close friends and community prayer groups started our prayer vigil for Luis.

As if the sky fell on my head, when two immigration officers knocked at our door at midday, showing details of a person's name, address and picture based on a photocopied passport, and asked me the question if this was the person that I'd reported missing! I was tongue-tied and about to collapse from shock and disbelief! I just cried loud bitterly and shouted to the Lord my burst of emotions, until I felt numb!

Through investigations and researches on Luis' record, he flew out of the country and went to Germany to meet his long-time high school sweetheart, whom he accidently found in SOCIAL MEDIA! These internet meetings and everyday communications had revived his feelings towards her, whom he also found her now as a widow. He desperately wanted to see her, hence, decided to meet her and leave his own family secretly! I nearly lost my mind because I couldn't handle Luis' betrayal and infidelity!

One day, I drove home and had an accident and landed in the hospital for few days. Jodie, being the only girl in the family was the one who looked after everything at our home and Jay, as the eldest made sure, that everyone was okay. Their daily visits at the hospital kept me alive and motivated. I went through counselling and was diagnosed with deep depression. Being a government employee in Human Relations Department, I was given an emergency leave as I was found to be mentally dysfunctional and not allowed to work under certain conditions. Our children Jodie and Jay handled the everyday food and miscellaneous expenses, as they were both employed now, while my work payment paid off our monthly mortgage duty.

My mental status took time to improve, until Luis appeared like a ghost! He was serious in leaving us and chose to live with his former sweetheart. We both decided to sell the house, as I can't afford to pay it by myself. Luis took off again! At this point in my life, where in all angles blew up to the roof resulted to my mental breakdown! I had lost my husband, injured in a car accident, had forced-leave at work, and our dream house was crushed into pieces like the sand castle washed away by the furious tidal wave! I was left as a broken woman in heart, soul and mind! I was transferred to a mental unit and stayed there for almost a year!

I knew that my loving children had fervently prayed for me, as well as my relatives, close friends and most especially our community prayer groups. Later on, I'd learned that prayer vigils were organised by leaders and also masses were offered for my healing. My children never failed to drop by for a daily visit just to see me and we prayed together. This kept me ALIVE!

Until one sunny and bright morning in Autumn, I woke up and immediately stood up, held my rosary and prayed to God! I felt like I just woke up from a trance or a dream! With tears in my eyes, I cried out loud as I had realised that I was in a mental unit in a well-known hospital! "NO!" I said to myself, "I shouldn't be here!" A nurse heard my loud cry and hastily opened the door witnessing my upset situation. I immediately told her that I shouldn't be at this place while tears kept flowing and kept on repeating to her that I shouldn't be here! She calmed me down and sat down with me and gently asked me this question, "Why do you think, you shouldn't be here?" I prayed to the Holy Spirit to give me the right words, in order to convince this nurse my normal state of mind. So, I gently held her hands with the rosary and told her what my work was before I ended up here and calmly, slowly narrated my sad and heart-breaking story. I found her completely immersed in my story until she was emotionally touched, as I saw tears in her eyes too. I stopped my narration and pleaded for help to get me out of this mental unit. She kept quiet for a while and then told me to fix myself, take a shower and dress up properly. I obediently adhered to her advice.

After morning tea, I was called by the Head Nurse of the mental unit and nervously knocked at the door and heard the gentle voice, "Come in and have a seat!" Much to my surprise, the Head Nurse happened to be the same nurse whom I met and had a long chat in the very early morning! I felt joy and hope in my heart, for I had intensely poured out to her the totality of my story. She had opened my personal file and gladly said that everything what I'd told her this morning had matched the statements in my record. She then immediately requested that I will be moved to the recovery unit which is helpful for the next journey of my total freedom from darkness!

I praise and thank you, Oh Lord God Almighty! As the praise songs were being played in the car, Jay, Jodie and Josh also sincerely expressed their thanksgiving to God through the songs. They were all in ecstasy and their hearts were filled with joy and overwhelming happiness for my final release! That was the happiest moment in my life, to hug, feel and kiss once more my children whom I thought I will never see again! They had given me these words of assurance and said, "Everything will be fine Mum! God is with us always and forever!" Amen, Amen, Amen!!!

We were all over the moon going home straight to the three-bedroom house of Jodie and cheerfully showed me my own room. I was surprised to see it so beautifully adorned with my favourite designs and colours, including the cosy bed, side table and chair. My sweet and loving children knew me very well!

My three children are now all married with their own respective families living comfortably in their own abodes. The family tragedy they had encountered in their journey did not stop them from achieving their goals because of their strong faith and trust in the Lord. I am truly a very proud mother of these three beautiful children, the only gems I have in my life, together with their respective spouses and my adorable grandchildren! I always looked forward for their rostered visits at my place!

With contentment and peace in my heart, I ended up living in a retirement village which I believe is a gift from God. Its proximity to my children's houses is a big bonus. I live here with some of my very close friends from our community group. Indeed, it is a very peaceful and safe place to live in knowing that I have the whole village, as my second family that I can rely on too, with their profound love and utmost care. Thank you Oh, Lord God Almighty to all Your blessings and graces! Praise to you Oh Lord! Amen!

Reflections

Oh my God! What a beautiful and inspiring story! What a strong woman of faith! Jovy's strength of character is truly unbelievable! She had managed to face all the trials and challenges in her life since her teenage life and became a mother at an early age. Her early emotional and mental struggles made her a resilient woman who hadn't lost her presence of mind. But, unfortunately had weakened her strength, when Luis, her second husband had unexpectedly changed his course in sailing because of the influence of social media! No wonder Jovy had trauma on social media, because it was a big factor in the collapse of their married life and beautiful family life as a whole! At this critical period of her life, she fell into a deepest pit of mental breakdown, because of too much truck-loads of burden which she wasn't able to carry. With this almost deadly fall, miraculously she was able to rise up again victoriously, through God's blessings and the loving support and prayers of her family, relatives and prayer groups of the community!

Social media have advantages and disadvantages in this modern world. Experts say that there are more good points to it because the world is moving so fast in all different angles, so society needs it for progress. People must learn how to use it constructively and wisely and must not be controlled by social media!

Jovy, together with her children didn't lose focus in achieving a good life, but rather were more motivated to do the best they can and prove to Luis that he made a big and grievous mistake in leaving this beautiful family, the ever-loving mother and faithful wife and the good and responsible children. Most of all, Jovy's strong love and faith in the Lord made a big impact in her life! Proven to be a model mother, who raised her children in the right direction and taught them the importance of praying to God at all times, no matter what circumstances they encounter! As what the famous quotation of William Shakespeare states, "All is well, that ends well." May God be praised forever and ever!

"Enter his gates with thanksgiving,
and his courts with praise;
give thanks to him and bless his name.
For the Lord is good and his love lasts forever,
and his faithfulness through all generations."
(Psalm 100: 4-5)

STORY 4

Single-Blessedness
Life is My Vocation

"Through him we are fully confident that
whatever we ask according to his will,
he will grant us. If we know that he hears
us in whatever we ask, we know that we
already have what we have asked of him."
(1 John 5:14-15)

My mother was in deep sorrow and kept crying every now and then, since dad's funeral. This was the sombre memory which kept coming back to me each time I go to the city, where we used to live.

I was six years old when my dad, an accountant in one of the taxation agencies in the city, died of lung cancer. Being a solo parent, it was hard for our mother to cope with the expensive lifestyle in the city. So, she readily agreed to her sister's practical suggestion. Soon after came the significant day of our lives, which to this day I can clearly remember! My mother, together with us: four girls and the youngest only boy went on an exodus from the city to the northern regional province of our country, upon the invitation of her sister to live with her in their ancestral home with her husband and only daughter Elsa. I was so excited to see my cousin Elsa, with a long and curly hair and can't wait to play with her!

When we arrived in the province, the very first in the list which mum wrote down was our schooling. Our eldest sister Susan and I, being the second child were enrolled in the parish Catholic School managed by the nuns. Mum kept on reminding us to thank God always because He loves us so much. God is always with us to protect and guide us, especially at this time we had lost our father. Providentially, through Dad's life insurance benefits, we were left with money to start a new life, especially in school tuition fees. Mum had started to practice her profession as a dressmaker in order to support our everyday needs and save money to achieve our dream of building our own house on the family's ancestral land.

Years went by so fast, all of us had finished high school. Sadly, our eldest sister Susan was in college when she was diagnosed with diabetes. Luckily, she managed to pass the requirements to be accepted as a working student in order to get free education in spite of the diagnosis. Our mother had worked so hard day in and day out being the father and mother of the family, in order to meet our daily needs. I took over on some odd jobs in our household, as Susan became weak and sickly. I'd noticed my mother's dependence on me more than our eldest sister due to her health condition, which I didn't mind at all. I loved helping her whenever she needed me around the house or for errands. I also availed the benefits of being a working student in the school's administration office for free education from high school until I finished my Bachelor of Science in Commerce.

Through God's graces and blessings, I immediately found a good job in one of the prestigious accounting firms in the city. It was my intention to be employed locally, so I could be near my mother and sickly sister, but of no avail, because of too many competitions in the job placements. You see, I was never fond of fashionable clothes and just simply put on my white blouse, plain skirt and neatly brushed hair with no makeup, as opposed to my opponents, who were all so pretty and elegant, applying for a bookkeeper's job. Some bosses gave more importance to the outside looks of a person, rather than the knowhows. That was the time when I got more motivated to move on to a higher level in the field of accounting. My days, weeks and months were all spent wisely in my further reviews and studies in addition to my weekend-stay in the province to spend time with my family.

Then came, the most awaited time in my life which was the board examinations to gain the title as a Certified Public Accountant. I was so nervous, but confident because I knew

I'd exerted a lot of effort and really burned the midnight oil in order to achieve my goal. Most importantly, I had full faith and trust in the Lord for His utmost help and guidance. After one month, the results of the board examinations were all written in the newspapers. Indeed! I passed it with flying colours! Praise God Almighty!

I stayed in the same company not because of the generous salary-package offered to me, but mainly because the management had impressively shown me their objectives and priorities of not looking at the person's outward appearance, but rather the inward goodness and worth of the person. To me, this is very precious! They had sent me out in different firms in our own province as an Auditor. To my surprise, I was given that company, whose boss had turned me down because of their wrong preference! I was nervous and prayed to God the right way to handle it. Vengeance or Forgiveness? I felt deep in my heart, that I must remain the same person, simple and humble, no matter how high were my achievements!

On that very day I had to visit this notorious company, the more I intentionally dressed so casually. Then the secretary came out and straight away said, "We are sorry, we have no jobs available." "Oh my God! here we go again!" These were the words, I said to myself! This time there was no presence of self-pity, but my heart was filled with joy and contentment with what I had achieved! I simply told her that I was sent by our Accounting Firm to audit their company. When she heard the word "audit" she became restless and nervous and totally lost control of what to do, until the manager walked in and the secretary hurriedly introduced me to him as an Auditor. I knew that she was worried that her boss might just ignore me just like what she did! They both treated me so nicely and I can see how hard they tried their best to impress me. Then I kept my peace and just quietly executed the right review as their Auditor according to the law of accountancy, government compliance and industry regulations, not according to my personal judgement! Thank you, Oh Most Holy Spirit for guiding me all the way! Thank you, for blessing me your spirit of humility, simplicity and forgiveness! I left the place with joy and peace in my heart!

After a span of five years, so many important events happened in our family like: Nelia, the third child in our family already got married and with a gorgeous baby girl Kathy; then Belinda, the youngest of the girls had graduated from college with the highest honours and the youngest, the one and only brother Peter had to wait for another two more years before college graduation too. Meanwhile, our eldest sister Susan just simply enjoyed her teaching career in our province and our poor mother had stopped her job as she was getting older and weaker. She stayed home contentedly and always looked forward for the visit of Nelia's family in order to play with her adorable granddaughter Kathy!

Life is not always a bed of roses, there are thorns on them! One morning, I woke up with a painful arm and tried to trace where the pain was coming from, until I felt a lump near my armpit next to my left breast. Straight away, I'd decided to see my doctor, who immediately referred me to a specialist. After all the x-rays, biopsy and all other tests, the specialist gave me the most devastating news that my left breast has to be removed due to the presence of some cancerous cells and might spread to the other parts of my body. I took an emergency leave from work for almost a year with the hope of recovering from this deadly disease! I fervently prayed for God's mercy and grace to overcome this fear and anxiety and He answered me saying, "Have no fear, for I am with you; be not dismayed, for I am your God. I will give you strength, and bring you help. I will uphold you with my right hand of justice." (Isaiah 41:10). Since then, this scriptural passage became my mantra! True enough, after one year I was in remission! I praise and thank you, Oh Lord God Almighty!

You may ask the question: How about my love life? Well, I had fallen in love too with a really loving and thoughtful classmate in high school named Jonas. But it ended merely platonic, like we were a brother and a sister to each other. We kept our relationship that way for so many years, until one day Jonas said good bye for city adventure and sadly, since then, I hadn't heard any news from him. I felt that my love life is my own precious family. I firmly believe that God calls every one of us for a mission and I definitely knew what my calling was! Let's see what unfolds in the next years of my life, according to God's plan!

Due to my mother's poor health, I was impelled to leave the company where I had worked for twenty years as an Auditor and had switched career into an instructress of accounting subjects in the college close by. This was only three days a week, because the other four days, I had to look after our mother. Then the good news was announced by our eldest sister Susan that she was getting married. Of course, we were all happy for her, but worried about her health situation due to diabetes. After two years, the next announcement was from our youngest sister Belinda's engagement party and planned to get married at the end of the year. We were all so happy for her future. Peter also had graduated from college and his current job made him a busy man.

All the happy and memorable events that had transpired in our family, were all replaced with the agonizing news that our poor mother passed away. Sadly, she just didn't wake up from her sleep. We were all devastated, most especially me! I vividly remembered the past few days before she died, that she often called me and asked to sit so close to her and kept telling me how she loved me. Her words had deeply touched my heart when she said, "Eloisa, my dearest daughter. I truly thank God for having you as my support all through the years. You patiently had looked after me and your siblings' welfare. You are truly God's gift to me, a very loving and caring daughter!" I cried so hard, but felt peace in my heart knowing that our beloved mother had gone to her eternal home in heaven, now reunited with our father. We all honoured her for being a strong and courageous woman of faith with full surrender to the Lord, superbly performed both roles of a loving mother and father to her five children! May her soul rest in peace. Amen!

Since our mother died, I pursued further studies in law while teaching part time in the University. Eventually I became a lawyer and I felt I was at the peak of my career when another storm came into my life. Peter, my one and only brother suffered from kidney disease and immediately required to undergo dialysis. Only him and myself were left at our ancestral home, because all of my sisters were all now married with their own respective abodes. So, I was impelled again to leave my job as a full-time lawyer and just be a part timer. This is again the call of duty to look after my brother Peter. Until he wasn't able to go to work anymore and had to stay home. I made sure that he had someone with him at home, when it was time for me to work every Monday, Wednesday and Friday. So, I hired a community nurse to stay with him on those days. It just worked out so perfectly and I felt so peaceful about the arrangements.

Then one midnight, my younger sister Nelia, with her only daughter Kathy surprisingly visited us! She hugged me straight away and poured out her emotional pain, while Kathy was crying too! I told them to calm down and I quickly prepared them warm drinks. Nelia sadly confessed about her husband's wayward ways for so many years, which she couldn't take anymore. She had decided to separate from him and he didn't even stop her. I felt so sorry for my sister and I totally understood her anguish. I lovingly prepared their bed and advised both of them to rest and we will talk in the morning. It took me by surprise when Nelia woke up so early and already prepared our delicious breakfast! She seemed to be calmer this time and emphasised again of not going back to her husband. Her daughter Kathy said that she wasn't happy being with her irresponsible father. I wholeheartedly welcomed them with open arms at our ancestral home. Life went so easier for me and especially with Peter. The community nurse was no longer required, as Nelia took over in looking after our sick brother. God works in mysterious ways!

Life is just like a roller coaster, particularly with emotions. All of a sudden, I received a shocking news that our eldest sister Susan died due to her chronic condition of diabetes. Again, I felt this sword of sorrow like when our mother passed away. Oh Lord, give me strength to carry this heartbreaking feeling!

We had all moved on to our lives and made sure that we gather at our ancestral home for catch ups every fortnight at least. So, Belinda and her family regularly came over for a whole day stay and spent quality time with each other, especially with Peter. Providentially, with my earning capacity, I was able to afford all the required medicine and miscellaneous expenses for Peter's dialysis!

Day in and day out, Peter and all of us had survived with our respective struggles. Mine and Nelia's were mainly emotional, but my brother's struggles were both physical and emotional. With that in mind, made me more grateful to be blest as a healthy human being, though with the scar of breast cancer! I know God will continuously bless my health situation, because Peter, my poor youngest brother desperately needed me in order to survive. Nelia relied on me too as an older sister to accompany her and Kathy towards the plan and will of God for them. God is an ever-loving and merciful GOD! I completely offered and surrendered ourselves to HIM our health, our lives and future. God is all-knowing and knows what is best for us! Amen!

Reflections

What a woman of pure heart and soul! Eloisa's virtues of humility and simplicity, with a loving and caring heart are all unimaginable! To me, this is a perfect story of a living saint!

From childhood till adulthood, Eloisa's life journey made her a very strong and resilient woman who was able to handle all the most unbearable situations in her life. Just like that saying, "Gold is tested by fire!" She had performed and executed very well all the most challenging encounters in her journey, because of her true faith and trust in the Lord.

From losing a father, a mother, her eldest sister, her personal battle with cancer, her struggle with people's wrong judgement on her appearance, her own emotional pain in love, her younger sister's traumatic separation from her husband, until this present physical state of her youngest brother suffering from kidney disease, undergoing dialysis -- were just all handled perfectly by this very simple-humble woman with a heart as huge as the sky in showing her profound love to her family!

Eloisa had realised very well from the beginning that God called her for a mission, this vocation of single-blessedness life, a spirit-filled life full of meaning and inspiration. Her life is so inspirational for others to emulate. It is truly instrumental to mankind to prove how God, with His Most Holy Spirit empower and guide people's lives in the right direction towards His kingdom, the very essence of our existence! Praise to you, Oh Lord God! Amen!

"The Lord is my strength, my shield; in him, my heart trusts. I have been helped and my heart exults, with my song I give him thanks."
(Psalm 28: 7)

STORY 5

The Sacrificial Love
of a "Mother"

*"Her sons rise up and call her blessed, her
husband sings her praises "Many women have
done wonders, but you surpass them all."*
(Proverbs 31: 28-29)

Roland and I, had joyfully celebrated our tenth-year
wedding anniversary in a thanksgiving mass in our local church,
followed by a luncheon attended by our immediate families. It
was a festive celebration of thanksgiving of our true love shared
faithfully together for ten years. It would have been the merriest
and happiest, if there were some children, or even only one
celebrating with us this memorable occasion. Sadly, there was
none!

Hope remained in my heart with firm belief that God
will touch us and bless us with a child, one day. We remained
hopeful and faithful like Hannah in the Old Testament, who

prayed for a child for many decades, and never gave up hope, until God answered her prayers and blest her with a son named Samuel, whom she offered to God to serve Him out of her gratitude. "For nothing will be impossible with God." (Luke 1:37)

Roland and I had chosen to stay in our province for we both loved simple life with fresh fruits and vegetables around us in our property, as long as we had planted seeds of different crops all year round, surely, there would be bountiful harvest at the end of each season! We couldn't ask for anything anymore because of our bounty and affluence. I taught as an elementary public-school teacher in our local school, while Roland worked as a clerk at the Taxation office in our municipality. Until, we both felt that there was emptiness in our marriage because of the absence of children. That was the time after ten long years, that we started to get checked for fertility. The doctor found no reason at all why we could not have a child. So, I started my novenas to all different saints for intercession and most especially to our Blessed Mother Mary. Every day, I faithfully attended mass in our church and prayed my novena.

Two years had quickly passed, until one morning, after my mass attendance, I felt dizzy and fell on the church ground. People nearby saw me and brought me in the nearest medical centre. According to the doctor, I was so pale as white as paper, so advised me to stay there at the medical clinic for further check-up. Roland immediately left work, when he was told of what happened to me! One of my co-teachers, Emmy visited me and said, "Oh, Annie, maybe you are pregnant!" Those were the sweetest words I had ever heard and hastily answered her, "Oh, I pray that those sweet words are from Heaven!" Roland hugged me so tight and we both prayed together with tears in our eyes and with full faith in our hearts that I could be really pregnant! The doctor then told us to come back after two days to get the result of my pregnancy test.

After two days, Roland and I took a day off, went to church to attend the daily mass and prayed together my novena. You may be wondering what is a mass and a novena? The mass is the highest form of worship in the Catholic Church, which ends in the celebration of the Holy Eucharist, while novena is also a form of worship which consists of devotional or special prayers asking for intercession and divine intervention. After church, nervously we went straight ahead to see the doctor. As soon as the doctor invited us in, I saw his eyes gleaming with joy and instantaneously felt that ecstasy and elation for I knew that I was pregnant! The doctor happily congratulated us! Out of our overwhelming happiness, we both hugged the doctor! And with tears of joy, we'd never stopped praising and thanking God for His goodness!

You can just imagine how careful I was in carrying this blessed baby in my womb. I will be forty years old, when I will deliver our baby, so I had decided to take two years leave just for precautions. Thankfully all the nine months went on smoothly, and I am due anytime for the baby to be out in this beautiful world! God is good and everything went normal with no dramas! A baby boy was born, and we unanimously named him Ronnie, as a combination of our names of Roland and Annie. He grew up as a healthy child, until he reached the age of ten, he got sick vomiting and lost his appetite. He was brought to the nearest children's hospital for thorough study. The doctor sadly informed us that there appeared a danger of a chronic kidney disease on his left kidney in the future, but at this stage, medications were available to help avoid the illness, with the help of the right food intake. Again, we surrendered everything to God and His holy will and asked for His grace and mercy. We fervently prayed for the Holy Spirit's wisdom and guidance to show us the right direction for the cure of our only son!

In the early 1980s, everyone in our school talked about migration to Australia. It was the talk of the town that this well-known "Land Down Under" and "Country of Opportunities" opened its door for family migration, but with educational qualifications and skills. When I heard about it, I immediately thought of Ronnie. Being a first world country, Australia surely is a top-notch in the field of medicine, so there is hope for Ronnie to be cured! Without hesitancy, Ronald and I had agreed to apply for migration and prayed fervently for God's will, if this is the right way to do for Ronnie's sake, He will make it all possible!

We waited patiently for the progress of our application and just surrendered everything to God. After six months, we received a letter from the Australian Embassy that we had passed the requirements, and stated that family migrant visas will be issued to us very soon! I praise and thank you, Oh Lord God Almighty!

True enough, the following year, we arrived in this new land of hope for Ronnie! Both Roland and I immediately landed on our specific fields of profession as a teacher and bookkeeper. It was so easy during those days, as Australia is just a new nation of only fourteen million in the early 1980s. Ronnie got enrolled in a Catholic school and we were able to secure our own humble dwelling after two years. Everything went on smoothly with our settlement in our newly found home and enjoyed the comfort of living and stability of our finances and most of all Ronnie's health. He had a regular check up with his very kind and friendly kidney specialist or a nephrologist.

When Ronnie had reached his university studies, he fell so sick and was rushed in the hospital. His left kidney disease had worsened to the point that he desperately needed a left kidney transplant. The hospital made an announcement for an immediate need of a donor! This process of getting the right donor calls for a lot of tests, like compatibility test, donor's kidney test and other requirements before a kidney transplant is to be performed. When Roland and I heard this, we understood the importance of each second and each minute in the serious condition of our son. Without hesitancy, I courageously and boldly told Roland that I will go to the Renal Department right then and there to volunteer myself as a donor and ready to be subjected to the different tests. Roland himself wanted to be a donor, but his chronic hypertension issue is a big deterrent to be a qualified donor. We hugged each other, then went to the hospital's chapel and fervently prayed to God and once again surrendered everything to Him according to His will. With tears in my eyes, I cried out loud to God, ***"Lord, with a grateful heart, I thank you for blessing us a son; I implore you to save him from death, as I donate my kidney. I am ready to give my life for him. I beg you Lord for your graces and mercy. Amen!"***

I opened my eyes from a very deep sleep, which I never had experienced in my life. I vividly remembered where I was in my dream. I ran and ran on an empty space filled with all lush of green grass as far as my eyes can see! Then I saw some people, young and old, men and women of all colours, strolling happily, and enjoying the beauty of the surroundings. They all saw me and just simply smiled at me. I didn't recognise any one of them! Until a lady in white uniform held my hands and asked me, "How are you feeling?" I simply said, "I'm okay, but where am I?" She signalled me to be quiet and just assured me that I will be alright. I felt a pinch on my arm and fell into a deep sleep again.

I woke up and readily saw Roland standing by my bedside and kissed me when he noticed that I opened my eyes and smiled at him. This time, I felt energised and strong! Then, the lady in white uniform walked in again and checked on my blood pressure and I'd noticed her gesture of relief! She quickly said that it's time for me to eat normally, but with soup diet only and gently removed all the attached cords in my arms. This time Roland slowly told me what had happened since I went to the Renal Department and volunteered to be a donor. With tears of joy in his eyes, he proudly said, "Annie, my dearest loving wife, you are a successful donor of your healthy left kidney given to our only beloved son! You had saved his life!" And I quickly uttered these words of thanksgiving, "Oh, my Lord God Almighty, praise to Your Most Holy Name! Thank you, Lord God, you saved our son! With your power and majesty, you saved us both!"

After three years, Ronnie officially graduated from law degree and continued further his studies for doctoral degree. He worked part time in a law firm and really worked hard towards his aim to pass the Bar Examination. Finally, with God's graces and blessings, he successfully achieved his goal and officially gained the title as a Lawyer. Ronald and I are so blessed with a son like Ronnie, an ever gentle and obedient son. Through his perseverance and determination, he is now a practicing lawyer, happily married with lovely Isabel and blessed with two healthy and gorgeous children, a boy and a girl!

All through the years, God manifested His great love and mercy upon us! We had surrendered all our prayers according to His will and they were all granted in His time! I'd volunteered to donate my kidney to our son and surrendered everything to His will, with a plea to spare the life of our only beloved son Ronnie! God is an ever-loving and merciful God! He lovingly saved us both! Oh, thank you Lord God Almighty, our Redeemer and our Saviour! Amen!

Reflections

Wow! I was absolutely dumbfounded with this heart-warming story of a loving mother with a sacrificial love! Annie had voluntarily donated her left kidney to her son, no matter what it costs, even her own life!

Generally, a mother's love is unconditional and never ending. The first priority and most important project of her life is her child. She is capable of giving her own life for her child, just like what happened in this inspirational story of Annie.

Have you ever wondered why mother's love is unconditional? Let me quote this quotation from St. Therese of Lisieux, "The loveliest masterpiece of the heart of God is the heart of a mother." Therefore, God, out of His own unconditional love, specially designed the mother's heart like His own! This is proven from this basic fact, that every mother who delivers a baby into this world, puts her life in danger. The newly born baby totally depends on the mother's milk in order to live. She sacrificially spends sleepless nights watching the new born for safety and free from any harm and danger. She carries out this role faithfully from the birth of her child until adulthood and still opens her ever loving heart at any time a need arises, no matter what it costs, even her own life! Her love is never ending!

Annie's inspirational story is a living example of a mother's unconditional and sacrificial love to her child! Her inner strength, absolute faith and trust in the Lord, and her total surrender to God's will are truly precious attributes to possess and to emulate. Indeed, this is such an amazing and motivational story which I am sure had touched everyone who had read this! May God be praised forever and ever. Amen!

"She is strong and dignified, and looks with confidence to the future. She speaks wisely and her words are kind. She keeps an eye on the conduct of her household, and does not eat her food in idleness."
(Proverbs 31: 25-27)

STORY 6

The Priceless Treasures I Earned from My Sacrifice

"The Lord will guide you always, he will satisfy your needs in desert places. He will strengthen your bones, and you will be like a watered garden, like a spring whose waters never fail."
(Isaiah 58:11)

It was the first day of my high school term, when I met Julian. He was a dark, skinny with medium height young boy, just a year older than me. When we were seated inside our classroom, he politely introduced himself as Julian and in turn I gave my name Miriam. From that day on, we were inseparable, together with some other two girls who were my neighbours. So, our group was composed of three girls and a boy.

Generally, high school days seemed to be the most exciting and unforgettable of all the stages in a person's lifetime. Why? It is a stage of easy going; a period of fun and adventure of teenage life. It is also the time of crushes and puppy love. Our group was always the subject of jokes by our naughty classmates, because Julian was the only boy following us around the whole day and every day. They constantly asked him, "Hey Julian, who is your puppy love among the three girls!" He remained consistent with his answer that no one in particular, because we were like his sisters. But they didn't believe him. So, our group just avoided the naughty boys, until we reported them to the principal and they were reprimanded not to bully our group again, otherwise their parents will be required to come for a resolution due to their misconduct. Since then, there were no more dramas and encounters with the bad group of boys.

Years had passed and we graduated from high school and moved on to college. Julian asked me what my plans were. I honestly told him, that I will stay in our province and study Bachelor of Science in Commerce. He told me his plans too. His father wanted him to see his uncle in the city, who will support him in his studies. That week, he left and I felt so lonely.

My other two friends also remained in the province and were enrolled as well with my course! I was so delighted to see them every day and really enjoyed each other's company like my real sisters. We all took seriously our studies because our parents spent a lot of sacrifices just to send us to college. With God's blessings, finally we graduated from college and every one moved on to follow her own destiny!

This particular day marked the most memorable day of my life, when my eldest sister Martha, together with her family had announced their migration to Canada. Due to her qualification as a nurse and her husband as a computer programmer paved the easy way to pass the eligibility test. The whole family rejoiced to this great announcement for their brighter future. Martha offered a mass of thanksgiving and invited some of our close relatives for fellowship. After three months, they flew to Canada to start a new life.

Meanwhile, my cousin Maria and I shared a room in the city, as soon as we passed the interview, which we applied as bookkeepers in one of the accounting firms in the city. The manager asked us to start immediately which we happily did. This was the start of another stage in my life. What a small world! Julian also worked in the same building, where I worked! Surprisingly, we bumped at each other in the corridor. I felt something different inside my stomach. I was so nervous that I couldn't look at him. We shook hands, and he instantly invited me for coffee. So, after work, we went to a nearby restaurant for early dinner. I was over the moon to see him once again after more than four years. He sadly told me that his uncle passed away four months ago and just in time for him to witness his graduation. His uncle had no children, so, he was the one who had supported him to finish his degree. Julian had a good job and lived at the old house of his uncle. The three-bedroom house had two spare rooms, so he decided to get them rented. He was doing well with his finances.

One Saturday, Julian visited me and my cousin Maria and invited us to watch a movie and dinner afterwards. But Maria said that she was not feeling well, and insisted that we must go. I was caught in that situation and could not utter any word, for I felt awkward to go by myself. But Julian was so quick to say, "Come on Miriam, let's go so Maria can have her full rest at home. We will bring her some food when we go home." Maria got excited about the food and said, "Okay then, I look forward for your surprise!"

That was the start of our blossoming relationship which resulted to some confessions during our high school days! Julian admitted that he was already in love with me at that time and I honestly told him that I had feelings for him too! One weekend again, he invited me and my cousin for dinner and requested us to dress up elegantly which we obediently followed. That particular night had completely changed my life, when Julian had given me a big surprise that never in my wildest dream would happen, as he gently knelt down and put a sparkling ring on my finger and said, "Miriam, will you marry me!" I nervously accepted his proposal and immediately planned our marriage the following year! I found Julian to be a very prompt and fast action planner-executor which is one trait I loved in him. True enough, we got married early January and I moved with him at his uncle's old house, which he later on owned.

After one month of our blissful holiday, Julian and I went back to work. That very first day back to work, I received a phone call from my eldest sister Martha and surprisingly said that she's in the city to see me! You could just imagine how elated I was! I told her to visit us and gave her our address. I was over the moon and can't wait to see her for I missed her so much: her kind words and advice full of wisdom and most of all her assurance that she always includes me and the whole family in her prayers.

It was so early in the morning, when I heard a knock at the door and my loving sister was standing there! We sweetly kissed and hugged each other for a long time while tears of joy kept flowing down our cheeks while uttering words of gratitude and praises to God! We haven't seen each other for more than five years!

I introduced Julian to her, who politely shook hands with her and asked her blessing as an elder sister, which Martha lovingly did! Then, she mentioned her own schedule to follow for the day, so, Julian and I can go to work and we all meet up at night for dinner in a nearby restaurant.

Martha, being our eldest sister became like the matriarch of our family, because our mother, who was very sickly and frail, depended so much on her on finances and any decision or transaction that the family may encounter. We had a very sumptuous early dinner and it was time for Martha to go back to the province to say goodbye to our mother and siblings. She had emphasized that she'd left me an envelope in my bag and I have to read it with Julian, and added that it was so important to read it after our night prayers!

Indeed, we followed Martha's important reminder. So, after our night prayers, we curiously opened Martha's long letter. It was an invitation for me to migrate to Canada, under her sponsorship. With my educational qualification, I can easily be employed and later on, be granted a residence visa. Then, once I become a resident, I can go home for my husband Julian and take him with me back to Canada. It really looked simple and practical, but I'd noticed Julian's hesitancy. Martha had emphasized that this is for the brighter future of our own family when we start to have children. This is a long-term plan to help as well our siblings, nieces and nephews to follow us in this beautiful country. Canada offers a better opportunity and stable standard of living. Julian didn't disagree with the proposal of Martha, but he asked me personally, if I would agree to it. He said, "Whatever your decision, I will abide." I kissed and hugged him with that answer, because he knew that I really wanted to migrate to Canada for the brighter future of our family. So, help us God!

After a very busy one whole month, my bags were packed and ready to go to the airport, with this feeling of confidence and faith that God is with me all the way. This is really hard for both Julian and myself to be away from each other after a very short time being together since we got married. But we both took it as a sacrifice for our future. I repeatedly told Julian, that I will be back for him, once I get my residence visa. I noticed his sad eyes, but he kissed me and hugged me so tight and said,

"Take care and I will see you in a year or two or even more. Lord God, help us!"

As soon as I'd arrived at the international airport of Canada, my sister Martha, together with her husband and daughter jubilantly waved at me and called my name! I ran to them, hugged and kissed them. My sister was in tears and couldn't believe how fast the plans went into fruition through the blessings of the Lord!

Martha had managed very well her time, as the head nurse of the geriatric's ward. Her healthy and active body kept her so quick in her walking, talking and executing different activities in the department. Through her diplomatic and good relationships with the other wards, she had enlisted me as a casual administration clerk in the children's ward. I was so excited to break this good news to my dear husband and so, I decided to inform him via long-distance call, though a bit expensive. I can't wait to hear his voice and pray together! I terribly missed Julian!

Because of my enjoyment and involvement in the children's activities, one month went passed so quickly. Until one morning, all of a sudden, I had stomach cramps, then vomited and felt so weak and dizzy. My fellow casual worker saw me in this situation, and so she hurriedly called a nurse. I was so pale and fortunately, my blood pressure was quite normal. They'd decided to do a blood test. Martha was informed about my condition and she did her best to get the results as soon as possible. After three hours, she went to my room and with apprehensive looks, she said, "Miriam, you are pregnant! Don't worry, you will be alright! For now, rest the whole afternoon and tonight after prayers, we will talk about it, okay?"

My sister led the prayers and mainly lifted me up to God for protection and safety in my condition and asked the Holy Spirit for wisdom to handle this situation. I cried and surrendered to our Lord God Almighty my worries and anxieties. I just let go and let God control my life!

After weighing all pros and cons in my present state, both Martha and I felt peaceful in our decision to stay until I give birth. Then when the baby turns one year, I can go home and get Julian, my husband to come with me, to be a complete family. I kept Julian updated regularly on my health situation and he in turn replied promptly with his emphasis that I take extra care and eat healthy for the baby's good health. On my fourth month of pregnancy, I felt like I had bigger tummy than normal, and this led me to have an ultrasound. With my sister beside me in the room, she uncontrollably uttered these words, "Oh my God! The babies are two! You have a pair of female twins, Miriam!"

My very first impulse was to call Julian via long distance! I can't really wait to hear his voice, so I could gauge his emotions! I called him, but the number was not available! So, I just quickly wrote him a very long love letter. After two months, I haven't received any reply yet from Julian and this made me so anxious.

But I thought positively, that he might just be busy at work and hoped to receive one soon. For the meantime, I kept myself busy at work. My very kind and considerate manager gave me light duties like planning the daily recreational activities for the children, as well as printing sketches for the drawing sessions of younger children. This kind of work had made me more excited and motivated to concentrate on my well-being for the sake of my twins.

With the graces and blessings of the Lord, I gave birth to my sweetest and gorgeous twins naturally! My sister can't help herself and said, "Wow, thank God for such healthy and adorable babies!" So many beautiful photos were taken by my brother-in-law and I'd requested him to mail them to Julian via express mail. At last, after two weeks, I'd received a reply from Julian which made me cry when I'd learned about his lung health issues. I felt guilty being a wife, for I wasn't beside him during those times of pain. He was apologetic for not telling me, because he didn't want me to worry. Now that I clearly understood his sudden silence, I felt so peaceful and contented. Our exchange of love letters had continued for almost a year and we both decided that when the twins turned two years old, I will go home. By then, Julian will be able to come with me to Canada and be a complete family! I fervently prayed to God to let this dream come true!

When the twins were one month old, I asked the help of Martha to arrange their christening. I was so fulfilled when that eventuated and were baptised with the names Cristina and Kirsten! I felt this overwhelming joy and peace in my heart after that spirit-filled christening Sunday, in spite of my pain of missing Julian by my side.

I needed a break from work in order to look after the twins. It wasn't easy to take care of two infants, so Martha also took her annual leave to support me for three months. It was such a big relief to get help and from three months onwards, I was on my own, but found it easier until they turned one year old. Martha's family had arranged a first-year birthday party inviting some few friends. Of course, I sent Julian those beautiful pictures and he was in tears when I spoke to him over the phone.

Days and months went so fast! I really looked forward to see Julian and next month, our twins will turn two years old. As we had agreed, when they had reached this age, I will go home and get him. That time came, but I kept it a secret in order to give him a big surprise. I bought my return ticket and Martha volunteered to look after the twins, while I was away for two months enough to arrange Julian's migration papers.

When I'd arrived in the city, I just noticed the same surroundings and atmosphere and no changes for the last two years, since I'd left the country. I told the cab driver to drop me at Julian's place, but to my surprise another lady of the house told me that she's a tenant and Julian had moved to another address with his wife and one child! Luckily, she got the address. I was dumbfounded with what I heard! I kept my cool pretending that I wasn't shocked at all. While traveling to the address, I recalled all what the tenant told me, and I was totally shaken with indescribable emotions and completely lost my mind. I saw the rosary dangling near the frontage of the car and I cried to the Blessed Mother Mary! The cab driver had noticed my sobs and sniffles, but I quickly said that I was alright. When we arrived at the place, I kept my cool and immediately saw a pregnant woman of my age with a little boy of almost two years old, who looked exactly like Julian, at the front porch of the house. I asked if this was Julian's house and the woman politely nodded and said that she's the wife. I almost stumbled on the ground with her shocking reply and told her in normal tone, "Oh, I am his cousin and just dropped by to say hello. I will come back some other day to catch up with him!" When I looked at the cute little boy, I thought of the goodies and chocolates I brought with me for Julian and straight away gave them to the mother. Then I signalled the cab driver to leave and gave him another address of my cousin Maria, just to stay for the night. "Oh my God! The beautiful dream had crushed into pieces!" Maria tried her best to pacify me for I didn't stop crying since I'd arrived at her house. I finally came into my senses and asked my cousin a big favour not to mention to anyone of my sudden appearance. I politely told her that I had to let go of Julian, because I felt sorry of the pregnant woman and the little boy. I thought I was more blest than them. The next three days, I spent quality time with my sick mother and siblings and openly told them what had happened and my firm decision to go back to Canada without Julian. To be honest, I was devastated, but I can still hold my head high because it wasn't my fault that my marriage was broken. It was Julian who cheated on me and couldn't wait for me! Or was it? For leaving him for Canada, exchanging him for better future? I really don't know. Time will tell…. Oh, Lord, help me!

In the early wintry-foggy morning, Martha picked me up at the airport. She waved at me with a bright red scarf, so I could see her. When I saw her, I quickly ran to her and hugged her so tight with my sobs and cries unloading my heavy chest which I tried to carry and now had burst into her loving arms. While going home, she told me happy stories about the fast and normal growth and development of Cristina and Kirsten as well as their cheekiness and cuteness. Their differences are now slowly visible and distinguishable even you don't spend too much time with them. They're identical, but have different features and characteristics. Then, Martha gently advised me to attend a retreat organized by the local church in order to reflect and be in total communion with God, while she's still on holiday, because of my unexpected early arrival. I absolutely agreed and gratefully hugged her tight for I badly needed a retreat for my sanity!

Days, months and years went by so unbelievably fast! Cristina and Kirsten were already in their university studies and one chose the medical field like her godmother and one chose the accounting field like me. Then I received a very sad letter from my cousin stating that Julian passed away due to lung cancer. I told the sad news to the twins, who knew all the story of their father. In fact, one school break, I took them home to meet their father. They are such the sweetest and forgiving twins, because they had forgiven their father and out of wisdom, one of them said that both of them didn't totally blame him for what happened! We all agreed to fly home and pay our last respects to Julian. I felt so sad and yes with some guilt in my heart. But I knew Julian had understood me during those days of discernment and most importantly, God too!

The twins had graduated from their respective degrees and providentially landed on good earning jobs, which kept them both so busy. While I still worked full time and devoted my Saturdays in service to our church and community prayer groups and Sundays with the twins and Martha's family. I am so overwhelmingly happy and contented with the outcome of my sacrifices, for raising my twins by myself and the support of Martha and through God's utmost care and providence! Truly, God never abandoned me and always stayed by my side!

God truly blest me with this pair of identical twins, two different persons with distinctive characteristics and traits, but both sweet and forgiving! They are my treasures in my life with the memory of my only love Julian, who's now in heaven. Indeed, through my sacrifice, I had earned these priceless treasures, no other than my loving family! Thank you Oh, Lord for your divine providence and guidance all the way. Praise you Oh God Almighty! Amen!

Reflections

What a strong woman of faith! Miriam is a model of humility, faithfulness and compassion! With her simple and humble ways, she had remained true and faithful to her marriage vows to Julian, the one and only love of her life! She had chosen a sacrifice of being away overseas for a short time for their family's better future, but her unexpected pregnancy had delayed her planned quick return to her husband. Julian's infidelity had deeply hurt her when found with another pregnant wife and a child! Miriam's faith and trust in the Lord had absolutely put her to the test! Inspired by the Holy Spirit, she had chosen forgiveness and compassion, instead of hatred and vengeance! She had totally let go of her own love for Julian for the sake of the other family. She had sacrificed her own happiness and earned the priceless treasures of her life, her sweetest twins!

Through Miriam's firm and steadfast love for God and her perseverance and patience being a solo parent had greatly contributed to her main objective: to successfully send her twins to school until college. God's providential blessings and generosity, financial difficulty had never been an issue in her journey!

God blest her with a loving family, her eldest sister's family and for sure, more to come as her own family will become bigger according to God's will and plan! What an inspirational story indeed! Amen!

"If I ride on the wings of the dawn and settle on the far side of the sea, even there your hand shall guide me And your right hand shall hold me safely."
(Psalm 139: 9-10)

Story 7

Our Calling as Family Carers

"Not only that, we feel secure even in suffering, knowing that sufferings produce endurance, endurance produces character, and character produces hope, and hope does not disappoint us, because the love of God has already been poured into our hearts by the power of the Holy Spirit who has been given to us."
(Romans 5: 3-5)

One rainy and humid day, unexpectedly Tim uttered these words, "When can we ever hear good news on your pregnancy test?" I hastily hugged my husband with the same feeling of disappointment towards the unsuccessful test result. After five long years of our married life, Tim and I really longed to have even only one child! It seemed that something must be wrong with either myself or Tim. We both agreed to see a reproductive endocrinologist (RE), commonly known as a fertility doctor. After two months of different tests, the pain of waiting for the results was a torture for me being a woman. I had a lot of anxiety and questions in my mind and almost lost my sanity with the thought that I am the cause of infertility! I wasn't sure if I could handle that depressing truth, that I can never be a mother of my own child! I honestly told Tim about my feelings towards this and he simply said, "Lilian, my dear wife, let's surrender everything to God and gladly accept whatever His will and plan for us!" I was deeply amazed by my husband's remarks! I suddenly felt ashamed of my own pride and ego. What an ungrateful and selfish individual am I! This was how I saw myself after I heard Tim's astounding words of faith and trust in the Lord! Tim had to say those startling words, in order to wake me up and alarm me of what would unfold tomorrow's visit at the fertility clinic. Those words definitely woke me up and I prepared myself for the worst scenario and positively thought of plans for a meaningful life. Before we left our house, we prayed for strength and offered everything to God's will. This time, I felt peaceful and ready to accept anything, through the power of the Holy Spirit.

As soon as we walked in the clinic, the receptionist politely offered us seats. The fertility doctor saw us and straight away, without beating around the bush, told us the issue of our infertility. I truly appreciated his frankness, better than too many words of explanations which to me is called the "torture of waiting!" The x-ray results showed structural problems with my fallopian tubes which cause obstruction in the fertility. By this simple one-sentence finding totally had conditioned myself to adopt a child. The doctor recommended IVF or In Vitro Fertilisation, but we honestly said that we cannot afford the expenses involved.

Life must go on! From then on, Tim and I dedicated ourselves on weekends in service to the church and spent more time with both sides of our families. We fully surrendered and offered ourselves to God's will and plan for us, as what Tim had said before!

My side of family isn't too big, with only six siblings, unlike Tim's fourteen's siblings! My father already passed away and left our sickly mother. We both felt that God calls us to be a family carer. So, Tim and I had voluntarily taken my mother at our three-bedroom house and looked after her. We opened a little food and grocery store, where my mother mostly stayed the whole day, which kept her busy happily talking to people and made her life meaningful. As a couple, we'd managed this store and added more items to it, until it grew. The rapid growth of our business had also helped us to sponsor some of our nieces and nephew's tuition fees in high school. Whenever our siblings asked for support, we never failed them. Since then, Tim and I felt the hands of God guiding us, which clearly affirmed the mission He planned for us, Family Carers!

Our calling took place again, when one weekend my elder brother Raul with his two little boys of six and three years old had suddenly visited us. My brother looked so haggard and sick. In fact, he was sick with high fever and I immediately gave him medicine to lower his temperature. He had cough and cold at that time, so Tim quickly cooked vegetable soup for him, while I took good care of his two cute little boys. After two hours, Raul said that he felt better after the hot soup, medication and sleep. But I felt something was wrong. I was about to ask about his wife, when with teary eyes, he told us that his wife left them. She apparently was fed up living in poverty in the city and went with a wealthy man and abandoned her children! My heart was broken and felt so sorry for the children's welfare. Both Tim and I looked at each other with the mutual understanding of keeping the two boys in our household, which Raul pleadingly asked from us to do! We agreed to adopt the children and told him to stay until he recovered from his sickness.

That was the start of a different journey in our life! Tim and I had instantly a complete family of our own with two children! That Sunday, right after church, we enthusiastically went to buy the two boys their new clothes and shoes, especially for the oldest boy Riley in time for him to be enrolled tomorrow in kindergarten. The young boy Ryan curiously asked if he was to be enrolled too! What a smart little boy! From that very moment I saw these two boys, I already adored them, as if they were mine. Oh, God! We know that You gave us these two boys to be our children to love and care for!

Days, months and years had quickly gone fast, Riley and Ryan were both so diligent in their studies which gave us so much joy especially with their outstanding academic achievements! Both of them, excelled in different subjects in their elementary school years until high school. What a shame for their biological mother, abandoning such intelligent and obedient children! Tim and I couldn't be any happier and prouder as foster parents to these children!

My brother Raul never failed to send us letters from the city, for updates about his life and also wanted information about his two boys, in spite of his new family. Since he left his two boys with us, he moved on in his life and found a good woman, whom he later on married and now have two children, a boy and a girl. I was glad to hear of his new happy family and his good-earning job too! Praise GOD!

Tim and I were both dressed elegantly, ready to watch this much-awaited event - the graduation of Riley in the university. I was over the moon, with tears of joy in my eyes, and could hardly believe the truth of what I was about to witness, the fruits of our love and care for our adopted boys – especially Riley's end of a chapter in his life and start of another! Ryan too looked forward for another three years and he would be in the same memorable situation. Tim and I had been blessed by God with these two boys!

One night, Tim's mobile phone rang and I saw his face so devastated and started sobbing and crying like a child! Sadly, my sick elderly mother-in-law passed away. We all went to the province and paid our last respects to Tim's mother. After the funeral, all of Tim's siblings had gathered and discussed about their youngest brother Leo, who needed a carer due to his health condition. He was born with down syndrome and at the same time with chronic diabetes. Eva, one of the nieces, who just lived next door was asked if she wanted to be Leo's carer and she gladly accepted the offer. Everyone went home to their own respective families and moved on.

You see the roller coaster of life, just kept going naturally. Especially with emotions, which is certainly, a part of life that after sorrow comes joy, then after joy comes sorrow. After the sorrow of my mother-in-law's death, came the joy of Riley's good news of his job acceptance in a prestigious company overseas. He was given the visa to travel as soon as possible. So, our family had gathered together for thanksgiving and a simple celebration. I informed my brother Raul about it and indeed surprised us of his sudden solo appearance. He was just happy to send off his eldest son for more blessings and safety in his travel. They hugged each other, with both of them in tears and it was me who can feel my brother's pain and guilt of giving his son away, but mixed with the emotion of happiness of the gain of what he gave up!

After the first death anniversary of my mother-in-law, we heard the terrible news that Eva, Tim's niece who looked after Leo had an accident and was brought to the hospital. She was found with a fractured bone on her left foot and would take time to heal. At this point, Tim's family had planned to look for another carer for Leo. Everybody contributed his own suggestion, until the elder brother suggested that Tim and I will take Leo home with us as a trial, if he would like the environment. Without any hesitation, we agreed and sincerely took him home with open arms! Now Leo is the big brother to our two boys!

After five months of Leo's stay at our house and officially a member of our household, the more Tim and I felt so blessed and contented with our fulfilled and purposeful lives. Being childless, and unable to have our own biological child, definitely is not a deterrent to stop us to live a beautiful, blissful and meaningful life. What matters most is the happiness, peace and joy of searching and following God's will and plan. For us, when we found God's plan, we readily grabbed it and that is: our calling as family carers, which we delightfully and obediently followed!

Thank you, Oh Lord God for your love, faithfulness and guidance all the way! Amen!

Reflections

Truly, this is such an inspirational story! A story of victory over emotional disappointments, and biological incapability. As the saying goes, "When things go wrong, don't go with it!" Yes, let's think positive! Just like how Tim and Lilian had thought of ways to have meaningful and purposeful lives after the sad revelation of their helplessness to have their own child. Most importantly, they offered and surrendered themselves to God's power and will. God took over and controlled the flow in their lives. They obediently followed the path where God directed them through their faithful and constant prayers. God poured all His graces and blessings upon them. He is an all-knowing God, who knows and feels the deepest desires kept in their hearts! God is a compassionate God, and granted all the heart's desire of Tim and Lilian, the ever-loving and caring couple! They faithfully obeyed their humble calling as the Family Carers through the inspiration and power of the Holy Spirit! May God be praised forever! Amen!

> *"We know that in everything God works*
> *for the good of those who love him, whom*
> *he has called according to his plan."*
> *(Romans 8: 28)*

Story 8

To Live a Happy Life is a Choice

"I keep the Lord always before me,
for with him at my right hand, I will never
be shaken. My heart, therefore, exults, my
soul rejoices; my body too will rest secure."
(*Psalm 16: 8-9*)

Rainy season in my country is the farmers' favourite time of the year for it is a season of planting rice and different crops! But the children dislike it because this means they can't go out to play! As they sing this famous song, "Rain, rain, go away, come again some other day. We want to go outside and play. Come again some other day."

When the children noticed that I heard them sing this song, they ran away for they knew and anticipated what I will surely say. I used to stop and explain to them the importance of rain to the world in general and they will cover their ears and hide.

It must be the other way around. Be happy when the rain comes and welcome the sprinkles of blessings from heaven!

You see, people's outlook in life differs. Bad things could be looked at positively or negatively. When things go wrong in life, some people go with it; some don't. When situations turn into lemons, some make lemonade; others chuck them away. I prefer to be a positive person, because I want to live a happy life. It wasn't easy, but I did! Do you want to find out how? Just continue reading....

As I passed through the narrow path in the fields carrying with me a basket of warm food for the labourers, I saw my best friend Ella who will be getting married next month and warmly wished her all the best in life and prayed for a bountiful start of a new life! She just looked at me and seemed to be unhappy! Then surprisingly, she ran to me and hugged me so long and tight! She shockingly uttered these words, "I wish the wedding won't push through! I was shocked and so I invited her to come with me and have a chat, for I felt that she needed to unload her heavy burden. She gladly agreed.

Ella told me the shocking truth behind the wedding. I just thought we're in the 20th century, not 1590s! Her parents' culture of matched-marriage is still very much alive in their family. When Ella was born, straight away her parents already matched her with this man she will be marrying next month. I don't like it too! I am blessed that our parents' ancestry had long-forgotten such culture and moved on progressively into the modern world. In this case of Ella, I just advised her to try her best to develop this important emotion of 'love' towards her future husband in order to be happy. I know it will take time, but in due course everything will be fine. Just do your very best and keep smiling. She was pacified after our friendly talk and I saw her sweet smile again. Deep inside my heart, I felt so sorry for her, because that's not easy! What I had advised her was "easier said than done!" I felt a bit guilty of the advice I gave her, but there is hope and I offered them both to God's graces and mercy.

Being the second youngest of a family of six children - four girls and two boys, I felt like always, as the second choice; taken for granted or not given much attention in the family. I'd noticed the focus was more on our eldest daughter and youngest daughter. I remembered the olden days, when my parents eagerly opened packages of clothes, given to us by our aunt from America and happily distributed the girls' dresses and I was left out! Mama said, "Oh, Elisha, so sorry that I made a mistake in counting out of my excitement!" I just smilingly replied, "That's okay mama! I have a lot of clothes anyway!"

On one very special occasion, our family must attend the ordination day for priesthood of our uncle, my mama's brother! Unfortunately, our father was sick with fever due to cough and cold. So, mama had assigned one of us to stay and look after our dad. Guess who was assigned? Yes, straight away she told me what I should do when dad's temperature gets above average. I kept calm and just obeyed peacefully.

Years had passed so fast like a whirlwind, and all of us had finished our college degrees. My parents were so happy and fulfilled that through farming they were able to send us all to school until college. It was indeed, a big achievement for them through God's providence. But two of my sisters got married after two years since they'd finished their studies! Guess who? My eldest sister and youngest sister! My parents weren't impressed with their early marriages, but they just accepted their destiny and prayed for their good future. Rose, the eldest and her husband had settled in the city to manage the business left by her husband's parents. Because of this financial stability, our parents gave them their blessings when Rose and husband had announced their plans. Meanwhile Roslyn, the youngest, married a foreigner from New Zealand. She met him in the hospital, where she worked as a nurse. Robert had an accident, and Roslyn happened to be the assigned nurse in the ward. And the rest is history. Now, they're happily settled in New Zealand and I'd heard the last news that Roslyn was pregnant!

It was so hot that day, and can't wait to be home after a very long tiring day at the office. My manager had noticed my challenges of dealing with our "high maintenance clients," so she considerately said, "Elisha, you may go home now after all your hard work today!" You see, my manager kept on telling me, "You're such a breath of fresh air Elisha!" So, with a big smile on my face, I left the office thanking her for an early dismissal of one hour!

At home, I'd heard sounds of people upstairs thinking who would be our visitors at this time of the day. It was only around three o'clock in a very hot and humid afternoon! Then I heard a cry of a baby and I quickly ran upstairs out of my curiosity! "Oh! Roslyn, Robert and Rosalie, their fifteen-month-old gorgeous baby girl had given us a surprise visit just in time for our dad's birthday!" I instantly said boisterously!

Mama had organised a big celebration for dad's birthday and the surprise visit of Roslyn's family! Our uncle priest was the main celebrant in the thanksgiving mass attended by our immediate family, some relatives and close friends. It was indeed a successful celebration followed by a luncheon at our property under the shades of tall fruit-bearing trees surrounding all around our two-storey house. My two brothers had arranged dining tables and chairs for the visitors. Then there were two long banquet tables covered with washed banana leaves filled with different kinds of foods cooked by our relatives as their contribution to the feast, as well as varieties of desserts and drinks!

Roslyn's family stayed another three days which really made the whole house so alive and vibrant with the presence of cheeky and cutie Rosalie. She made us all happy and occupied the whole time they'd stayed. I just adored her so much! On their last day, Robert and Roslyn, much to my surprise invited me to visit New Zealand as a tourist. If I would agree, upon their arrival in New Zealand, they will sponsor me as visitor for three months. I instantaneously liked the offer, but first I have to ask our parents' blessings. Then our mother came into the scene, as I'd gathered that she must have known this plan already. She lovingly said, "Elisha, our dearest daughter, our sweet and humble one, you've been the sweetest of all, with no complain, no questions asked, just simply an obedient child! We love you so much and you deserve to see other places and see what fate brings you to another country. Your father and I, certainly, give you our blessings and may God be with you always." I hugged and kissed both of them, with tears in our eyes for finally I'd heard loving words from them and words of recognition, especially from mama!

After two months, I'd received a letter with an attached form from Roslyn and Robert to be submitted to the New Zealand embassy and immediately apply for my passport. All applications went through very smoothly, and all I had to do was to wait for my tourist visa and ticket! I prayed to God that if this is His will and plan for me, everything will happen so quickly. True enough, after two weeks, my visa arrived and ready to fly in New Zealand the following week! So, help me my dear God!

Wow! I straight away fell in love with the country! Its perfect sceneries are just breath-taking from its vast and towering blue mountain ranges, to sandy radiant beaches, countryside lakes and picturesque towns! I just loved everything I see around me! Yes, from the very first day of my tour around I absolutely felt that I found a second home. And I certainly looked forward to be with gorgeous little Rosalie every day. I felt so peaceful in my heart!

On the last month before my tourist visa's expiration, Robert's side of family invited all of us, including me for a family gathering. They'd also invited some of their closest friends to meet me. While having our lunch at their beautiful backyard overlooking a small lake, I'd noticed a man maybe in his late fifty's looking at me! I can clearly see him from my sun glasses. I became a bit nervous, so I went closer to my sister Roslyn. Then all of a sudden, he sat beside her and said, "Oh Roslyn, this must be your sister Elisha that you were telling me coming to visit New Zealand? She's prettier than you!" My sister, readily replied, "Oh yes, she is!" Then after the introduction, she asked for an excuse to do the baby's diaper changed. I felt so awkward being alone with Sonny and just in time Robert had joined us! Thank God for that! Then after our sumptuous lunch, we all had tea and more chats, until Sonny sat beside me. I'd noticed that those seated closer to us had stood up ready to go and they'd politely said their goodbyes. But Sonny remained seated comfortably and continued talking to me. He started to ask some personal questions, which made me so uncomfortable. I was thankful of Roslyn, calling me to help her pacify Rosalie, who had a little tantum. "Whew! Thank you for saving me!" I whispered to her ears! And she just laughed!

The day of departure was so dramatic and full of surprises. Roslyn told me that she was offered a high-paying job as a nurse in one of the hospital closer to home and desperately needed me to come back after two months to help her with the baby. Because I became so attached now with little Rosalie, I immediately consented to her kind request!

After a year, Rosalie celebrated her three years old birthday party attended by some group of families with children of her age. She was so active and happy especially when she blew the three candles on her beautifully decorated cake! The whole day went so fast and I felt so tired too after the long day of entertaining eight little kids! I mainly organised the little games and activities, as Roslyn was busy entertaining the parents. Then, as I was about to retire for bed, Roslyn knocked at my door to say thank you for the successful birthday celebration and said, "What will I do without you! A million thanks to you my dearest sister!"

One dramatic event happened during the family gathering of Robert. Again, I went with them to assist Roslyn on the hyper-activeness of Rosalie. Much to my surprise, Sonny was there too! It was at this point that Sonny honestly opened to everyone without secrecy that he fell in love with me and ready to spend the rest of his life with me. He was charmed, especially with my ever-smiling eyes and jovial spirit, at the same time captivated by my calmness and peaceful nature. Sonny was divorced ten years ago and didn't think of marrying again, until he set his eyes on me. Then strikingly, without any hesitation, he knelt in front of me and opened a small box with a precious ring and said, "Dear Elisha, will you marry me?" And the rest is history! It was a like a hurricane kind of romance, so fast and furious! But I thought this was better than Ella's marriage, because here I had the choice to accept the proposal or not! Yes, I must admit, when I first saw Sonny, I already had a soft spot for him!

As I had reminisced the past twenty-eight years we'd spent our lives together, I felt myself so blessed, though I encountered hardships and challenges. Sonny was seventeen years older than me, so we weren't blest with a child. Out of wisdom, I thought of God's goodness and knows deeply what is in my heart! It would be so traumatic for a child to grow up with a drunken father! You see, one thing I'd learned with Sonny right after our marriage was his alcohol addiction. I didn't know about this! If ever I'd known this before, I could have rejected the marriage proposal. Again, I suddenly thought of my best friend Ella, whom I'd lost contact since she got married. I wondered if she'd followed my advice. I wish she did! With me personally, I wasn't impressed with Sonny's drinking problem, but I followed my own advice given to Ella. I did my very best to work on our marriage. It wasn't easy, but through prayers and my full trust and faith in the Lord, I was able to handle Sonny. You see since he had retired, due to his weak legs, he just stayed home and watched television while drinking, until he got drunk and had fallen asleep. The big challenge was that part of him being drunk, and shouts at the top of his voice with bad words coming from his mouth! Sometimes I had to cover my ears, but what I used to do, was to turn on our cassette tapes with joyful songs of praises; wipe his face with warm towel; give him coffee, until he kept quiet and fell asleep. That was our routine every time he got into that bad moment. I fervently prayed for God's miracle that one day, his alcohol addiction will be totally wiped out!

Until, one day upon my arrival from my part-time work, Sonny was in severe pain and vomiting too. I dialled triple one and after ten minutes, an ambulance came. He spent one week at the hospital and the doctor found his damaged liver due to alcohol! The doctor gave him medications and told him that if he wants to live longer, then he must stop drinking! After a month of alcohol-less life, Sonny secretly drank alcohol when I wasn't around and I wondered where he got them from. Then, once again he complained of his severe chest pain and I called an ambulance. Sonny had survived his heart stroke and stayed in the hospital for two weeks. I was at his bedside one night and was in tears praying for his healing. The next day, he was released by the doctor and had given him some medications for his hypertension.

When he almost turned eighty years old, I'd organised a thanksgiving mass followed by simple lunch at home with my prayer group in the community. Sonny was so happy and said to the group that God gave him such an ever-loving wife and a very joyful person! He said, "I haven't met such a happy person in my life like my sweetest wife Elisha, who's always with a smiling face ever! I wrote all this to Roslyn, who had moved to Canada when Rosalie had turned ten years old and sent her so many pictures of Sonny on his birthday. I just expressed to her my joy of Sonny's recovery from heart stroke!

My life with Sonny had been a struggle, but I'd learned that in the midst of sorrow, one can still be joyful! I did my very best to be happy by thinking all the good things I have in life. Also, every morning I made sure that my cassette player was turned on with non-stop songs of joyful praises to the Lord. Until another unexpected incident happened with Sonny. He woke up one morning and said that his eye sight was so blurry. So, I took him to an eye specialist and he was diagnosed with glaucoma which caused his blindness of his left eye. The nerve which connects the eye to the brain was damaged due to high eye pressure. That very night, as I prayed the rosary before bed which I always do, miraculously Sonny said, "I want to join you in your prayers to GOD!" I hugged and kissed him with tears of joy that finally, after long years of waiting for him to join me, he was touched and accepted God as his God! Praise to you, Oh Lord God Almighty!

After two years of a happy, peaceful and prayerful life with Sonny, he had his third heart stroke and sadly, this time he didn't survive it. I was able to get a priest to give him final blessings and my ever-faithful prayer group stayed with me every night during the nine days novena for the soul of Sonny. May his soul rest in peace! Looking back at my life, indeed to live a happy life is a choice! I'd chosen to be joyful, in the midst of sorrow, because to fret over it, I won't gain anything, but to be joyful, I gain the victory of a peaceful spirit! I praise and thank you Oh Lord, my God! Amen!

Reflections

What an amazing life journey! Elisha is a remarkable woman of faith and endowed with the gifts of joy, cheerfulness and wisdom! She had shown possible ways how to change unpleasant and sorrowful situations into a happy and jovial atmosphere! That is not easy to do, but through the power of the Holy Spirit, everything is possible!

It reminded me of a priest's homily on one Sunday's live stream mass which struck me with his beautiful analogy of the word 'happiness.' With his cheery and gentle words, he said, "Happiness is like a butterfly, the more you chase it, the swifter it eludes you. Be still, and it just comes to you and may even sit on your shoulder!" What a striking imagery created out of his reassuring analogy! The more you reflect on it, the deeper it gets into your heart and soul and wanted to own it! This is precisely Elisha's golden choice, which she walked through all the way her life's journey. Whenever she sees the dark clouds in the sky, she knows soon the sun will be shining through for her! Every time heavy rain comes, she expects a rainbow to appear in the sky! What a great attitude to emulate!

From childhood to adulthood, until this present time of old age, she faithfully remained in the same spirit, still the same vibrant and jolly mature-woman with the strong faith and trust in the Lord! Indeed! to live a happy life is a choice!

"I keep the Lord always before me, for with him at my right hand, I will never be shaken. My heart, therefore, exults, my soul rejoices; my body too will rest secure."
(Psalm 16: 8-9)

STORY 9

Noble Role as a Family Provider

"Abraham named the place 'The Lord will
provide'. And the saying lasted to this day,
on the mountain the Lord will provide."
(Genesis 22: 14)

As far as I remember, my high school graduation day was the happiest day of my life! Why? I felt that, it was like climbing a high steep mountain! I struggled to reach the finished line; I battled the strong winds, dangerous storms, heavy rain and the scorching heat of the sun. It was a glorious victory when I finally made it to the top – I had graduated from my secondary education!

Being the eldest in our family of six children – five girls and one boy, Dad kept telling me, "Dinah, my dear daughter, I sincerely request you to look after your mum and siblings when I'm gone!" To keep him happy and remove his worries, I promised him that I will faithfully fulfill his request. I suddenly imagined Dad as the king putting on my shoulder the responsibility as the family's provider in his absence. It just saddened me the thought of losing him and felt anxious and nervous on the coming role, he bestowed upon me!

I had witnessed Dad's sufferings of chest pain and shortness of breath with unending cough. He suffered from emphysema in his late forties and never recovered from it. He wasn't able to continue his job as a carpenter and therefore, unable to support my school fees. The little amount of Mum's earnings from selling fruits and vegetables were just enough to meet our daily food and essentials. So, Dad asked help from his cousin Tessa, who owned a food and grocery store in town. The next day, Dad told me that Aunt Tessa had hired me as a helper in her store after my school hours from five o'clock in the afternoon till nine o'clock at night and the whole weekend too! Straight away, I thought of where would be my study time and doing home works? I was only on my first week in second year high school! With patience and perseverance, I worked as a store helper right after school. After three years of hurdles and long jumps, just like in the Olympics, I finished the line with a gold medal awarded to me!

After that happiest moment in my life, two weeks after I'd experienced the saddest moment! Dad died due to his long lingering disease of emphysema. I was devastated and heart-broken, but I had to be strong for Mum and my siblings. Life must go on! That was the start of my deeper and closer relationship with God and the Blessed Mother Mary!

With the schooling of my siblings, I had managed to send two of the girls in high school. My full-time work at Aunt Tessa's grocery store had covered their tuition fees and the other three siblings were still in the elementary education which was funded by the government. Mum continued with her little business of selling fruits and vegetables in the market, which she said had kept her busy and helped her a lot in her deep sorrow on Dad's death. Every one of us had moved on in our lives.

The next unexpected episodes in my life had dramatically changed our way of life as a struggling family. My very close friend since high school Nando, all of a sudden had expressed his love for me. He said, that I was his first love and ready to marry me! He was offered a good paying job overseas and proposed to marry me, before he leaves the country for one year! Of course, I was shocked with that very abrupt proposal and indeed very unromantic! I had a mixed emotions of joy and sorrow! Joy because a man had noticed me as a woman worthy to spend the rest of his life with; sorrow as I thought of his misjudgement of our family's struggle to be so desperate and marrying him would alleviate all our hurdles! I maintained my poise and gently didn't accept his kind proposal. He left without saying a word and from then on, I haven't heard from him at all.

After my surprise encounter with Nando, another very attractive proposal was offered to me! Aunt Tessa's long-time plan of business venture in America finally was approved and she needed someone to accompany her. The existing grocery store will be managed by her sister. So, being single, young, healthy and energetic, she had chosen me to be her aide. I was dumbfounded and unable to think of what to say, and she immediately said, "Dinah, being with you for four years, I'd known and tested you and you had passed all my requirements. So, I needed a positive answer from you and let me talk to your mother about it." And she left in a hurry to attend an important meeting, as if she knew that I won't reject her generous offer! Honestly, I cried with tears of joy and suddenly thought of Dad and my promise to him! Oh! thank you, Lord God for this blessing!

When Aunt Tessa had announced her proposal, I saw everyone in the family jumped with joy, except Mum. Oh, my poor mother – I knew what she would say and I felt the sadness in her heart! She said, "Tessa, you know very well that Dinah has been my support since Pablo died, and now you intend to take her away from me!" Aunt Tessa gently explained to Mum the good points and opportunities in our family especially my siblings' education, if she would give me her blessing. With sadness, she finally gave in, so, I hugged and kissed her, together with my solemn promise of regular calls and letters.

Time went so fast because of my busyness and tight schedule in managing this well-known fashion boutique which Aunt Tessa had applied three years ago. Since its launch, never we had a quiet day. The shop was always full of people enjoying the different garments from Hongkong, Thailand, India, Indonesia and also lately included the Middle Eastern clothing. Aunt Tessa was really a genius in knowing people's demand of their own particular clothes for she knew that America is depicted as a "melting pot nation." It is a country of diverse cultures and ethnicities that blend together as one nation. I truly enjoyed my job as I loved fashion too!

Meanwhile, my two sisters had graduated from their college degrees and were now all employed. The other siblings are still in high school and one will graduate the following year. I was so delighted to know of all their diligence in their studies, but saddened with the news of Mum's deteriorating health situation. So, I made it a point to talk to her, as well as see each other through Skype, one of the earliest inventions on modern communications. When I promised to see her on a weekly basis, I saw her face lit up and gleamed with joy!

One busy midday at the shop, I went out just for a quick lunch, when unexpectedly I saw Nando! I tried to hide, but he was about to enter the shop where I was waiting for my order. He saw me straight away and said, "Oh, what a small world Dinah! Really great to see you here!" He immediately invited me to sit on a spare table which was so hard to get at that time of the day, so, out of politeness, I just gave in. He told me of his business venture on renovations and really doing very well with his American business partner. Then, he started to talk about the same topic where we got separated. I just honestly told him, that this is not the right time to talk about this and besides I am in a hurry. So, he agreed and said he will pick me up for dinner tonight after work at 5:30 pm. Oh, my God! I don't know whether to say yes or no to that sudden invitation! So, just to be civil, I said, "Okay."

Even busy at the shop, my mind was full of different scenarios like a rolling camera in the movie. I immediately prayed for God's guidance and direction, if ever Nando would propose again! I can't help it but tell Aunt Tessa about my predicament, as she has been like a mother to me too. She just simply answered me to follow what makes me happy.

It was four thirty in the afternoon and in half hour, I will be closing the shop. At this time, I must have a firm decision on what answer I would give Nando. I was questioning myself, "Do I love him? Yes, I do."

So, on the dot, Nando arrived to pick me up and we decided to eat in a nearby restaurant, so we can just walk. It was a cold windy afternoon, and as a gentleman, he took off his jacket and lovingly put it on me. He knew that this was an instant dinner date, that's why I didn't have a jacket with me. I love his chivalric-gentle ways! We went inside the restaurant, and he instantly chose a nice peaceful corner. He gave me the menu folder and ordered our dinner. While waiting for the food, he started to tell me of all his achievements since he arrived in America and now very ready to start his own family. He proudly mentioned of his stable family in our country, whom he had supported for four long years and now it's his turn to be happy.

I immediately congratulated him for all his accomplishments and that he absolutely deserves to be happy! He immediately responded to my praises and said, "But you are my happiness!" My face blushed with that unexpected, straightforward and flattering reply, as the waitress arranged all the delicious looking food on the table and said, "Enjoy your food!" So, we got busy with eating and the conversation was more about the food on our table, which I prefer to talk about for now!

It was indeed a delicious and sumptuous dinner, which I enjoyed! I felt myself at ease with him and definitely had identified the firm answer I will give him. The menu coming next is coffee for him and tea for me with its famous warm churros with chocolate! As we were enjoying our dessert, here we go…., he started the conversation by asking me on what my plans are for now. Oh, my God! He definitely made it so easy for me to tell him exactly what I had decided to do. I slowly and gently said, "Nando, to tell you honestly, when you left me four years ago, you took my heart with you!" Wow, he was shockingly elated with that! I continued, "Now after four long years, never had I thought to see you once more, but had bumped at each other again. This must be God's ways, so that there will be a closure to the unfinished instant and shocking marriage proposal you'd offered me. You had done big achievements in your life and had supported generously your family and now you deserve to be happy. Again, I was flattered when you lovingly said that I am your happiness. Nando, tonight I am asking you to return my heart you took with you and find another loving heart who can love you wholeheartedly and fully! At this present time, my own family desperately needs me, especially my mother and to them all, I dedicate and give my whole loving heart! You greatly deserve the best woman who can completely love you and be with you the rest of your life! I have this big responsibility bestowed upon me and I will keep that promise until I die!" With that, I cried, as my tears kept flowing down my cheeks and he gently wiped my face with his freshly ironed white handkerchief and hugged me so tight. He totally understood everything what I told him, as I saw tears in his eyes too. I wished him all the best in his future and so did he, as we kissed and hugged each other lovingly like brother and sister! He then called a cab and dropped me at Aunt Tessa's place. Again, we kissed and hugged so tight for the last time!

That night, after my night prayers, I was in tears for opening my heart to Nando and felt absolutely peaceful in all that had transpired over that instant dinner date! I thanked and praised God for His guidance and wisdom upon me during our confrontation. I fell asleep quickly and slept like a log the whole night!

Days, months and years went by, all of my younger siblings had finished their college degrees and already employed with good salary. My two sisters are already married with two children each. Eagerly, they had invited me for Skype one Sunday, and I was over the moon upon seeing my two gorgeous nieces and handsome nephews, as well as Mum's glowing face with happiness and pride of being a grandmother of these lovely children!

This coming Christmas, I planned to go home and spend the festive season with my family and do it as a surprise especially to my dear mother. The next two years will be my retiring age, so I started to draw my plans what to do when that time comes. I really looked forward to my homecoming and started to buy clothes and some goodies for my siblings and the little boys and girls!

That was indeed my happiest Christmas, but it saddened me to see Mum's deteriorating health. One night, she told me, I wish that you won't leave me anymore, with tears in her eyes! I was touched with that and can't help but cry too! I lovingly kissed and deeply hugged her so tight. I couldn't sleep that night, so I stood up and made myself warm drinks and prayed again for guidance. Then I dreamed of Dad with his face gleaming with joy and said to me, "Dinah, I am so proud of you. You kept your promise and fulfilled my request!"

I woke up with peace and joy in my heart with that beautiful dream! It kept me more motivated to continue working and prepared myself for retirement in two more years. Then, after the festive season, I was ready to fly back to America and again Mum lovingly repeated her request for me to stay and don't leave her anymore. This really broke my heart, as I answered her, "Not too long, my dearest mother, I will stay with you!" And I left with a heavy heart.

Aunt Tessa had noticed my unusual movements and gloomy facial expressions and asked me if something was wrong. I instantaneously hugged her and burst out my emotions of sadness. I told her about Mum and my guilt of leaving her again. I know that financially our family is now very stable and we can all live comfortably even if I leave work right now, and enjoy my early retirement. Then she generously gave me a day off and spend the whole weekend on a retreat at the convent nearby to give me enlightenment on what to do. The more I hugged her, for I desperately needed some spiritual directions.

The retreat master was a Capuchin priest from the Order of Franciscan Friars known for their virtues of humility and simplicity. He gave a teaching about the purpose and meaning of life. He explained about man's priorities in life, would it be power, wealth, fame or family? He asked all of us ten participants to be in silence for one hour in front of the Blessed Sacrament and talk to God alone. He gave us our individual time slot in every hour solely with God! I said to myself, "That will be amazing!" During my turn, I poured out everything to God my inner thoughts and feelings, though I know that God is all-knowing! I felt that God is telling me, "Dinah, my daughter you had successfully accomplished the role given to you, as the family provider in the absence of your father. What are you waiting for? It's time to spend time with your mother.

Life is too short!" After an hour stay with God, I knew straight away what I will do after this wonderful retreat. It was indeed an eye opener for me! I thanked God for leading me in the right direction and I absolutely felt peaceful in my decision inspired by the Holy Spirit!

Aunt Tessa was so happy to see me relaxed and glowing with grace! I told her directly that I will be only staying until the end of April and going home for good, just in time for Mum's eighty-fifth birthday celebration in May. That must be her most precious birthday gift, that I will be with her always and not leave her anymore. Aunt Tessa was so happy for me, but will surely miss me so much. Her eldest daughter took over in managing the business, because she herself had retired five years ago and seemed to be enjoying her retirement, though she's always in the medical centre for check-ups.

The much-awaited time had come into fruition! Finally, I'd landed safely on the grounds of my cherished native land and to my beloved family, especially with my dearest mother forever! As I had mentioned, mother's eighty-fifth birthday was the happiest moment of our lives being a complete big family of twenty-one people and that includes my siblings' spouses and children. You can just imagine the glow on our mother's face, with her tears of overwhelming joy as she had clearly, and very slowly spoken the words, "I love you all dearly my children! First of all, let us thank God for all His graces upon us and for giving us your eldest sister Dinah, who had faithfully supported us all the way as our family's provider through God's love and divine providence! Your father's spirit is with us rejoicing on this memorable day and everything that had transpired in our lives!"

Life is too short! After four years of quality time with my sickly mother, sadly she passed away due to influenza infections. We had great time together and most especially I had all the time to look after her, feed her, bathe her and dress her up like a baby. I will cherish all those intimate moments we were together all my life! With God's mercy, her death ended her sufferings and gone peacefully to her eternal home and reunited with our father!

Though deprived of a husband and my own children, I absolutely felt a fulfilled and accomplished woman with the noble role given to me and lived a meaningful and purposeful life with God's grace and guidance! I felt loved and respected by my siblings and their spouses and truly enjoyed the precious moments of fun with my nieces and nephews. I couldn't ask for anything anymore!

With my own spirituality, I volunteered as a catechist in our parish public schools, a rostered reader of the Liturgy of the Word on Sunday masses and a church cleaner during weekdays. I enjoyed staying in the church and spending more time in the Blessed Sacrament. I thank God with all my heart for all His guidance and protection all through the years! Praise God Almighty! Amen!

Reflections

Wow! Dinah is definitely the beloved heroine of the family as the sole provider! The early loss of her father as the family's bread-winner had impelled her to take over the role. She is a perfect example of an obedient, responsible, faithful and dedicated daughter!

What else a parent could ask for a child? Her loyalty and faithfulness to her treasured family is incomparable! She had sacrificed her own love life for the sake of the responsibility bestowed upon her by the dying father, which she had sincerely, faithfully and lovingly fulfilled!

Indeed! What a noble role she had successfully accomplished through the grace of God! She is likened to a sacrificial lamb, who had given up her own happiness for her beloved family. What a selfless act! She had reaped the golden reward of forever peace and joy in her heart! What an amazing woman of faith, love, sacrifice and humility worthy of emulation! She walked through a very meaningful and purposeful life truly inspired by the Holy Spirit! May God be praised forever! Amen!

"May the Lord bless you and watch over you!
May the Lord let his face shine on you, and
be gracious to you! May the Lord look kindly
upon you, and give you his peace!"
(Numbers 6: 24-26)

The Pain and Glory of Having Stillborn Babies

"Know that the Lord is God; He created us, and we belong to him; We are his people, the sheep of his fold."
(Psalm 100:3)

With the presence of the priest inside the ward, made my broken heart restful and felt the hands of God on my shoulder with His peace and comfort, but I can't help but cry out loud the pain and anguish of my soul for the death of Joshua, an eight-month-baby inside my womb! Yes, I was induced to deliver a stillborn baby!

When I felt the severe pain in my womb, Joe called triple zero and I was rushed in the closest hospital. The emergency department team sent me straight to the birthing ward and immediately gave me labour induction for an emergency delivery of my beloved baby! I can feel what's happening with my poor baby Joshua! Joe and I had already named our baby as Joshua, the appointed successor to Moses, with the thought of him as the last of our children. "No matter what happens during the term of this pregnancy, I will keep him, Doctor!" These were the words I firmly uttered in response to the shocking news from my obstetrician. I clearly remembered her words, "I'm so sorry to give you again the unpleasant results of the ultrasound, Evelyn and Joe. The picture had reflected a baby with the "Edward syndrome!" Being familiar of this kind of syndrome, so I cried bitterly and poured out my pain, while pounding my chest and questioned God, "Why Lord! What have I done to suffer this pain! This is the second time Lord! Why me? Why us, Lord? Why?"

Joe and I were high school classmates and later on became sweethearts when we finished college. It's a norm that parents do not allow their children to be involved in love relationships while studying. Their emphasis on the importance of education was sort of a mantra to all the children and repetitions on the ban on love relationship sounded like a broken record! Together with my three sisters, we were raised by our devoted Catholic parents to be prayerful and never failed to attend Sunday masses. They had instilled in our hearts and minds, the love and full trust in the Lord.

I personally obeyed my parents, because I love and respect them. Joe had already expressed his love for me in high school, but I said that we just remain friends and let destiny work on us. True enough, we both finished our college degrees and both found good jobs which made our parents so happy and proud of us. Because we stayed in the same locality, it was easy for us to meet and communicate. Joe repeated his expression of love towards me, which I had lovingly reciprocated. But we remained pure and chaste as we both believe that it is not right to have sex before marriage. Honestly, we were able to stick to that promise until we got married!

I had witnessed through my parents' jovial reactions that overwhelming joy of knowing that soon they will be grandparents! Yes, Joe and I had visited them straight away as soon as we'd learned about the good news of my pregnancy. My mother immediately went to the altar, lighted a candle and we all prayed for the safe growth and delivery of the baby. God is good! After nine months, I gave birth to a very healthy boy, whom we named Jeremiah. He grew up so fast and just remained a very happy and healthy baby until he'd reached his first birthday! I had organised a thanksgiving mass, followed by lunch at our newly built house with Joe's side of immediate families and mine. Jeremiah's first birthday celebration became unforgettable for his struggle, but with persistence in blowing his first candle!

Joe and I never believed in taking pills as a form of birth control. Being a nurse, I know all the different side effects of taking drugs inside one's body. If ever there is a baby coming, so be it - a blessing from heaven! This is what we both firmly believe! True enough, after six months from Jeremiah's first birthday, I fell pregnant! Joe was so excited to know the baby's gender and kept on telling me to do the ultrasound. For some reason, this time I wanted to remain it as a surprise for all of us, just like in the olden days. But Joe never stopped convincing me, until I gave in to his request. On the third month of my pregnancy, we visited the same obstetrician, who gladly welcomed us and immediately did the usual check including the ultrasound. She told us to come back after a week, or if there was something urgent, she would call me earlier. Just after two days, she called us to visit the clinic as soon as we can! Why? There must be something wrong! Oh Lord, please save my baby!

Before going to the clinic, Joe and I went to the local church and fervently prayed for our baby. We prayed for strength to accept whatever lies ahead of us; to abide by God's will. We left the church light-hearted and strong to face anything. As soon as the doctor saw us, offered us cup of tea or coffee and again, I felt nervous with that very gracious welcoming gesture! So, politely Joe and I had both tea, which made me think that I might need it. She asked us to sit and slowly showed us the picture of the baby and explained the meaning of everything and all the expectations that we will face. Then she gave us this option of abortion! And I cried loud, with a very quick response of the word, "NO!" For few minutes, I cried bitterly with the comfort of Joe's words, "Don't worry Evelyn, we will keep the baby and let God control his life!" The doctor heard that and she just agreed to what we had decided.

Yes, I knew all about Edward syndrome! It is a genetic disorder in babies which causes severe disability which affects the child's growth and development. It is associated with chromosomal disorder with abnormalities in many parts of the baby's body. In fact, I'd seen pictures of babies with such deformities and also my doctor had shown some too, just to sort of tell us the possible appearance of the child. She had further explained that defects in organs are often life threatening for both the baby and mother. We requested the doctor to stop and emphatically said that Joe and I can't kill our baby! We had offered and surrendered him to God! We are ready to face this big challenge in our life. Our plea to her was to rigidly monitor us both and we're ready for check-ups anytime needed.

After nine full months, I contracted normally which was a good sign. Then I fell asleep. I dreamed of some tiny cries of a baby coming from the clouds and I tried to reach him and carry him in my arms, but he said goodbye and flew up higher and higher in the sky. I cried in my dreams and woke up with tears flowing on my cheeks! I'd noticed that everyone around me was sad and suddenly I felt Joe's hands and hugged me and said, "Josiah is now with God and the angels in heaven!" Oh, I felt numb and speechless! Then I asked the question if someone had performed an emergency baptism. Then Joe quickly answered that he did and named him Josiah as we had agreed. "Oh my God Almighty, I know Josiah is with you and he is one of your angels in heaven! He is the baby who appeared in my dream!" Thank you, Oh Lord God, my Saviour!

"Jeremiah will be awarded the highest honour in his kindergarten class!" were the welcoming words of Joe as soon as I entered our lounge room and ready to rest my aching feet. Then when I heard those motivational words, I felt so excited and my tired body became so strong and alive again! "Oh wow, where is my smart baby?" Then Jeremiah hurriedly ran to me, kissed and hugged me. I said, "I'm so proud of you, my darling boy!"

That night, I felt different in my body. I seemed to be so tired and lifeless. Then Joe suggested that we both take a day off and visit our local doctor. At the clinic, we'd met our former classmates in high school and had a quick catch up while waiting for my turn. Then I felt so sick and asked excuse from them and hastily went to the restroom. When I came out, weak and pale, the doctor called me for my turn. He straight away took my blood pressure which was normal and took urine sample, followed by instruction to come back tomorrow for the result that I might be pregnant!

When I heard the word 'pregnancy,' I felt a sudden pain in my heart due to the traumatic experience we had with Josiah. But every time we think of him in heaven, my emotions suddenly changed into peace and joy. That morning, I was ready to hear the result of my test, whether pregnant or not! Joe was with me for moral support and just called his boss that he'll be a little bit late. It was so fast because the receptionist just gave me a letter from the doctor with the result inside. The doctor was called for an emergency home medical service. Joe opened the letter and saw the big letters of "CONGRATULATIONS!" I'm pregnant for the third time!

Praise God! Everything went on smoothly with my third pregnancy. Both Joe and I became faithful to our daily prayers and masses for the baby's health and successful delivery. I was so careful and had extra precautions to be free from any form of sickness. Just days before my full term, Joe rushed me straight in the hospital when my bag of water broke, a signal for the baby to see the world outside! God is good! A healthy baby boy, whom we named Jacob was born! Praise to you, Oh Lord God Almighty!

Our house became so much alive and vibrant with the presence of another baby boy in our family! The grandparents on both sides regularly visited us and looked forward to carry the little bundle of joy! Truly, Jacob is another God's blessing to us!

Days, months and years had quickly passed without any dramas. All of Jeremiah's and Jacob's check-ups regarding their growth and development were all normal. With God's blessings and graces, they grew up healthy and smart kids. Joe and I offered masses of thanksgiving for all of this peace and contentment that we are enjoying.

This year, I'll be turning forty! Joe had mentioned one time that he would organise a big party for me! But I refused to hold a big celebration for myself, but instead, I thought of joining a fund-raising event for a good cause, which Joe gladly agreed. I humbly asked my relatives, close friends and workmates to sponsor me in my "Walk for a Cause" to be donated to the Cancer Research Foundation. That was my 40th birthday celebration which made me so overwhelmingly happy, especially when I'd learned that the raised-funds had exceeded my expectations! Praise God!

After a week from that very fulfilling and meaningful event, I felt so weak and always dizzy. Joe drove me to the medical centre and the doctor immediately took my blood pressure, blood test, as well as urine test. He told us to come back in two days. Meanwhile, Jeremiah and Jacob joined some children's activities on weekends and just made our time so occupied, but of course happy and enjoyable. So, the following day, both Joe and I decided to take a day off for the results of my medical tests. For some reason, I felt so anxious about this. As usual, we made sure, we'll be able to attend mass before going to the medical centre in order to replace my anxiety into peace and comfort.

Without beating around the bush, the doctor directly said, "Evelyn, you're pregnant! This is your fourth pregnancy and you're on your forties, so I strongly recommend that you take extra precautions. A monthly check-up with your obstetrician is highly advisable!"

After three months, Joe and I went for the scheduled ultra sound check on the baby's gender and development. Again, the same feeling of anxiety overtook my whole body which made me sick and ran to the rest room to vomit. I felt so weak and pale, when again, my regular obstetrician sadly broke this devastating news that symptoms of Edward syndrome were clearly shown on the baby's features! She definitely knew of our stand to keep the baby no matter what, so she straight away calmed me down and sincerely committed a rigorous monitoring on both the baby and myself.

Days and months had quickly passed. I remembered the whirring sound of the ambulance with Joe's firm hands holding mine, seated beside me praying the rosary. I heard his repeated prayers, "Oh, dear Lord God, I beg you save Evelyn and Joshua!"

The sight of the priest inside the room had immediately pacified me, for I knew that Joshua was baptised and now an angel. I just kept quiet after the loud cries I burst out of my chest and asked God's forgiveness for my questions and doubts. Then I fell asleep. I dreamed of Josiah and Joshua wearing white clothes; hand in hand, they were strolling along a narrow path surrounded by lush green grass and beautiful flowers, happily waving at me from afar, and called out, "Mother! We love you!" Then, they'd joined the other children in white clothes too, until I can't see them anymore! I truly cherish that beautiful dream and from then on, I loved to recall the details and always I felt peace and joy in my heart!

Joe and I had moved on in our lives, though from time to time still feel this pain of having stillborn babies. But with this painful experience, we found all the bright side of it, most especially God's great love to us. We firmly believed in the sacredness of life and we let God controlled the lives of Josiah and Joshua. With God's wisdom, He took them up to His Heavenly kingdom to be His angels! This is the greatest reward that Joe and I had reaped from our faithfulness and full trust in the Lord! Oh, thank you Lord God Almighty! Praise to you forever and ever! Amen!

Reflections

Wow! What an outstanding couple with strong conviction on the sanctity of life! Different people have different views about abortion. This had been a very sensitive issue and a popular topic for debate as far as I remember since 1970's. It became a longstanding controversy due to its moral, legal, medical and religious aspects.

Evelyn and Joe had shown an exemplary advocacy on the rights of the fetus to live! Being both devoted Catholics, they believe that human life is sacred, holy and precious, as man bears the image of God. As proven to their painful and agonising experiences of two babies with Edward Syndrome disorder, they'd strongly continued the full-term pregnancy and totally surrendered the babies' lives upon God's loving hands. They had absolutely let God to be in control on the lives of their two precious babies no matter what kind of disability or disorder they were in during those very challenging moments in their lives as parents! Their strength of character is just so powerful and mighty! Their faith in the Lord is as solid as a rock! Their life journey was truly remarkable, with their strong and firm convictions worthy of emulation! This is such an outstanding story truly inspired by the power of the Holy Spirit! Amen!

"This Good News shows us how God makes people upright, through faith for the life of faith, as Scripture says: The upright one shall live by faith."
(Romans 1:17)

Story 11

The Blessed Life of a Caregiver

"Those who do not take care of their own,
especially those of their household, have denied
the faith, and are worse than the unbelievers."
(1 Timothy 5: 8)

I come from a big family of twelve children – eight girls and four boys and had experienced the struggles and hurdles in securing our daily food, school fees and other family essentials. But I can proudly say that our parents were the most hard-working parents I've ever seen in my life! Dad was the number one wholesale buyer directly from the farm. He was always the very first customer lined up in buying fruits and vegetables as early as two o'clock in the morning every day. By the time he arrived home, Mum had already prepared their very early breakfast and ours included. After their simple meal, off they go to the nearest market to sell all what Dad had procured at dawn. This was their daily routine with no fail, as far as I could remember. Mum never missed to see me first before she goes and gently whispers, "Rosalia, my dearest, God be with you for looking after your brothers and sisters!"

Being the eldest among the girls and second eldest of all the children, I was the right hand of Mum in the kitchen. Laundry was shared among the other older girls and the house/backyard cleaning was assigned to the boys. We worked as a team, because our parents were out earning money for all our needs from two o'clock in the morning until three o'clock in the afternoon. All of my younger siblings had treated me like their mother, which I didn't mind at all and in fact, I loved it! With this role, given to me, I barely finished my elementary education. When I'd learned to read and write a bit, I just simply lost interest in my studies; found more enjoyment being at home; looked after my younger siblings, and cooked for our big family.

Time had passed so quick and I didn't realise that our eldest brother Joel had already finished his college degree! Once again, I was asked by our parents if I wanted to continue my studies, and I just simply answered a negative response and told them I enjoyed being at home. But honestly, I was ashamed to be in school again and be teased by the naughty and mean children as 'the old girl'.

Our eldest brother Joel became an accountant in one of the prestigious accounting firms in the city and earned good money. He had helped a lot in the school fees of the younger siblings who were mostly in high school. Out of his concern towards my future and well-being, he had convinced me to study even only a vocational course of my choice. So, I studied dressmaking course for one year. Our parents were so happy and contented with what had transpired in our family, and never failed to thank me for all my help and support in the household chores and most especially in looking after my younger siblings.

Our simple life became prosperous, as everyone had shown great love and devotion for whatever each one was doing, whether in studies, or household chores. Our parents had trained us to be mindful of each other with love and respect. Their deep love for God was the main legacy that they'd taught us and instilled in our hearts and minds. Sundays had always been the special day with God and family togetherness.

Until one day, Joel had announced a very significant news which had changed our lives dramatically. He was sent by his company's senior accountant to manage their existing accounting firm in Adelaide, Australia. Our parents gathered us all and prayed together for thanksgiving for all God's endless divine providence!

Joel immediately left after one month and had started a new life. He regularly called us for updates through Skype, so he can see us all. One time, he broke again a surprising news that he will go home in the following year and marry his girlfriend, Marian, whom he met in college! We were all happy for him for he was already in the right age to get married. My other siblings were so excited, because they had also their own girlfriends and boyfriends, but can't tell our parents, because the eldest wasn't even married. You see, even in marriage, our parents believed in family hierarchy protocol! My siblings kept on pushing me to attend gathering and parties, so I can meet other people, but I preferred to be home. Home, with my family has always been my blessed sanctuary and my only love!

Joel and his loving wife Marian had quickly settled down in Adelaide. With both of their good paying jobs, they were able to secure their beautiful dwelling and had enough savings to start their own family. Then, when they'd attained their citizenship, one by one, they were able to sponsor their own siblings to migrate too! On our side of family, Joel had sponsored all our siblings who had finished their college degrees. Until six out of the twelve children were all approved as migrants and had quickly settled in Adelaide. The next step that Joel did was to sponsor our aging parents and that included me as their designated carer, in order to quicken the process. True enough, with God's grace and blessings, the application was approved and the next thing I knew, we were all reunited in this beautiful land of abundance and opportunities!

I then became the most in-demand sister! Aside from being the carer of our aging parents, my siblings had assigned one child per day to be at our humble dwelling from 7:30 am till 5:30 pm. Our parents were so happy and looked forward to see, play and take care of one grandchild every day. I really thought that with their joy and happiness with the grandkids had greatly helped in the longevity of our parents' lives. That arrangement had worked perfectly for all of us. My siblings were so generous in giving me monetary assistance, which I refused to accept, so they did it differently. They had opened a bank account for me and there appeared their generous and kind assistance as a gratitude in taking care of their children. They kept repeating these words, "We are so blessed for having a loving sister like you, who had looked after us when we were little and now our own children! You deserved a lot more than what we give you! We love you so dearly, sister Rosalia!"

Every Sunday was our family day. After Sunday mass, we used to gather at one house in which Joel had organised in a rostered basis. You could just imagine how many we were all together breaking bread from different dishes cooked by every household, the endless catch ups and afterwards, watch the games of the children! You see my six siblings were all married with at least two children each. Honestly, I'd lost count every time we'd met of at least twenty-five of us all in all! You could just imagine how happy were our parents shown through the glow on their faces, mixed with the tears of joy!

Days, months and years had quickly passed and there were no more little ones. They had all finished high school and some were in college. At this time, our aging parents had both shown some signs of deterioration in their movements, as well as in appetite. The doctor had mentioned that they had aged normally with no health complications. The weakening of their bodies was due to their old age. Their love for one another had never faded that even in death, was all manifested. Both died peacefully in their sleep. Dad passed away one year earlier than Mum. They're both gone to their eternal home prepared for them by our Heavenly Father. May their souls rest in peace! Amen!

Being alone now, I'd spent a lot of time in the church cleaning and arranging the flowers on the altar. I'd joined prayer groups in order to keep my whole week busy and looked forward for being with some sisters praying together and having fellowship with them. The usual Sunday family gathering was retained and everybody looked forward to see each other and updated each family's activities, just like the memorable days when our parents were with us!

One morning after mass, I'd started my usual cleaning, when an old man asked my name and gladly said that he wanted to help in cleaning too! Of course, I can't say no to that, so I just let him. After cleaning, he invited me to have coffee in the local coffee shop close by, which then I'd refused and just made up some alibis. Then, he said, "Oh, okay, I understand. Maybe next time." And we parted ways.

That night, I felt a bit guilty for telling a lie to the old man and asked God's forgiveness during my night prayers. Very early in the morning, I went to attend mass and continued my voluntary cleaning. Unexpectedly, the old man appeared again and helped me. After cleaning, he invited me for coffee and this time I agreed and felt peace in my heart. That was the start of our friendship!

Gianni, was an Italian born widower with two children both married and lived in Perth. Twice a year, they made it a point to visit their father, who refused to leave Adelaide and preferred to die here and rest with their mother, who died of breast cancer three years ago. These were the confessions of Gianni, and I'd related to him my life story too. We'd met regularly right after our voluntary church cleaning for coffee, just like old time friends! With this new found friendship with an opposite sex, was the first time in my life ever, so I'd decided to share this news with my siblings on one Sunday gathering with apprehension on what they would say! To my surprise, they'd all clapped their hands for joy! Joel said, "Oh, dear sister, we're so happy for you to have found someone! You deserved to be happy! Please invite him on our next gathering, so we can meet him!" Then, I simply replied, "Oh, please don't get me wrong, he's just a friend to me!"

The following Sunday, all my siblings and their respective families were so excited to meet Gianni, as I can see on their faces! Then, I was surprised with Gianni's thoughtfulness, because he brought fresh flowers and cake too! All of a sudden, the whole house was filled up with lots of blown up pink and white balloons! Oh, I shockingly exclaimed, "What's going on?" Then Joel stood up in the middle and warmly welcomed Gianni! He had confessed that Gianni had inquired on the where abouts of the eldest brother in our family and had requested to meet up with him! He said, "I found Gianni as a very respectable and gentle person and certainly, happy for you Rosalia, if ever love would blossom in your friendship! When you had shared about Gianni to the whole family, we already knew about him! That's how we love you dear sister! You had shown your great love and care to all of us including our parents and our own children! So, it's our turn to look after you and make sure that you are in safe hands!" I can't help but shed tears and became so emotional. Then Gianni immediately pulled out his white handkerchief and wiped my tears! At the same time, on his aching knees, which he could barely hold on, gave me a precious sparkling ring and uttered the famous words, "Rosalia, my dearest, will you marry me?" The rest is history!

At the further north of Adelaide was the beautiful cottage of Gianni, overlooking a luscious vineyard which he had managed for ages until this present time, but had leased it to some younger families nearby due to his old age and ongoing lingering sickness. The place was almost one-hour-drive away from the residence of my siblings. So, with the Sunday gatherings, we were excused, because Gianni can't drive anymore. They just visited us from time to time or Skype each other for updates.

I was so happy with Gianni being a very gentle and loving person who kept on telling me, "Rosalia, my precious one, I haven't met such a very loving and caring person in my entire life other than you! God must have given you extras when He gave away these virtues to His people!" I had kept those sweetest and loveliest words in my heart forever!

Being married to Gianni for three years was so precious to me. I had cooked his favourite food and spent time praying together and recalling every detail of how God allowed us to meet and blest us with this sacrament of marriage regardless of our old age!

You see, Gianni didn't let go of his long-time faithful worker Raphael, who's also of his age, with his own family residing at the back of the cottage. Raphael had served him for almost forty years now and had truly shown his faithfulness towards Gianni.

One evening, Gianni had complained of severe chest pain, so I immediately called triple zero and also called Raphael for help! In a minute, he was there beside his long-time master and tried his best to resuscitate him, while I held on Gianni's hands and fervently prayed to God to save him. The ambulance had arrived and took over and rushed him in the nearest hospital. But sadly, Gianni didn't make it to the hospital! "Oh, my dear God, why? You could have saved him! Why Lord?" I bitterly cried out loud with all my questions to God!

I cried again of disbelief and I was totally devastated, as my siblings' presence had pacified me. They had comforted and reassured me that they will not leave me alone. A priest came to bless Gianni and his lifeless body was taken away. I heard God's words saying, "Rosalia, don't be sad, but rejoice for he's gone to his eternal home in the Heavenly Kingdom with me!" With those reassuring and loving words, I felt peaceful and joyful. Then I opened the door of my heart and came out those sweet words of Gianni whispering to me, "Rosalia, my precious one, I haven't met such a very loving and caring person in my entire life other than you! God must have given you extras when He gave away these virtues to His people! I thank you for your unconditional love and care!"

I had moved back to Adelaide proper and had lived contentedly in a retirement village in a one-bedroom unit. I have devoted my remaining years to God, by voluntarily cleaning the church and arranging flowers on the altar and spend quality time with my siblings and their respective families. With my little pension, every Christmas, I had made sure, that all of my siblings' families had one sack of rice and some little goodies and chocolates for their children. I felt that my life as a caregiver was truly the plan of God for me, for I feel fulfilled in my life. The path that I had walked through the years, truly had manifested the love, peace and joy of Christ! Amen!

Reflections

Truly! what an absolute loving and utmost caring woman! Rosalia is indeed a classic model of these two virtues! Because of her closeness to God, she easily found her calling.

Since childhood, her mother had already known of what kind of life her eldest daughter would lead. Indeed, she had followed the right path towards God's will and plan for her.

Being single can be one greatest blessing in life, as shown in Rosalia's life. She had reached her eighties, with a very fulfilled and meaningful life!

There was a twist in her life of being a married woman briefly for three years and had felt being loved and cherished by a gentle and kind man named Gianni. Again, being a loving and caring person, as she was innately endowed with, had strikingly affirmed by the sweetest words she had ever heard in her life from her short-lived husband Gianni, "Rosalia, my precious one, I haven't met such a very loving and caring person in my entire life other than you! God must have given you extras when He gave away these virtues to His people! I thank you for your unconditional love and care!"

It seemed that Gianni's role was God's messenger to pronounce Rosalia's gem-like virtues of a truly loving and caring woman; a virtuous woman of love and a dedicated caregiver throughout her life!

"If anyone enjoys the riches of this world, but closes his heart when he sees his brother in need, how will the love of God remain in Him? My children, let us love not with words or with our lips, but in truth and in deed."
(1 John 3:17-18)

STORY 12

An Ever-Forgiving Heart

"Bear with one another and forgive one another, whenever there is any occasion to do so. As the Lord has forgiven you, forgive one another."
(Colossians 3: 13)

"Before the sun goes down, see to it, you have forgiven anyone who had offended you and in turn ask forgiveness to everyone you had offended knowingly or unknowingly." These were the words that I'd learned from my religion class teacher Sister Therese since I was in the elementary grades, which I tried to follow till my adult life and old age. It wasn't easy, trust me. As that saying goes, "Easily said than done!" I will share with you the story of my life regarding forgiveness.

My parents had two boys and my dear mother fervently prayed for their third child to be a girl. And her prayer was answered when she gave birth to a gorgeous baby girl and named her Elena. And that's me! But the tricky part was that, I didn't grow up with my mother and father, instead I was raised up by my Aunt Lilia, my father's sister who had lived a single-blessedness life. I was her star and angel as she often called me, when I was a little girl. I loved her dearly like my real mother!

When I had turned into a teenager and mature enough to understand about life's complexities, I became curious about the mystery behind my parents' relationship. I didn't stop bugging my dearest Aunt Lilia and asked questions like: Why don't I live with my parents like my two brothers? Why don't I see my father at all? Why doesn't he visit me like my mother? My poor Aunt Lilia wasn't sure what to answer, so she played safe and said, "Elena, time will come for the answers. I myself will tell you without asking me. Just wait for the right time."

So, from then on, I just kept quiet and just concentrated on my studies, until I had reached college. In the college campus, I had met my oldtime playmate Andrew, a very happy-go-lucky guy, but really smart! He was so good in numbers and I had a crush on him! He often visited me at home just like a friend and made our home works together. Aunt Lilia knew him very well and always happy to see him around with me. She was aware of Andrew's family background as one of the most respected families in our town.

Being my trusted friend, I told Andrew about my concerns, especially these many unanswered questions in my mind. So, I had asked him to accompany me to my parent's house during daytime, in order to make sure that my father won't be around.

He agreed to help me and so we visited my mother. Of course, my mother was surprised to see me with Andrew! I hastily introduced Andrew as my classmate and friend, which was the truth! She hurriedly grabbed me inside and asked Andrew to watch outside if ever my father comes. The whole two hours quickly had passed, and I went out of the room in tears. I hugged and kissed my poor mother, who was also in tears and in turn kissed and hugged me so tight. She uttered these words to Andrew, "Please look after your friend, Elena, my dearest daughter and take good care of her!" I felt a bit embarrassed about her words implying deeper meaning on my relationship with Andrew.

The truth about the extra gifts endowed generally to mothers had clearly manifested in my two hours one-on-one with my poor mother. Mothers are gifted with this strong Extra Sensory Perception or commonly called ESP. They also are known to have the sixth sense, always one step ahead from anyone in the family in terms of insights or perceptions. They are also endowed with intuition, which is a strong feeling of something unknown, which later on, they could mysteriously identify with no fail!

On our way back home, I was so dead quiet. I felt numb and lifeless, until I couldn't hold my tears and burst out on Andrew's consoling shoulders. Then he said, "Whatever it is that upsets you, please remember I am here for you! If you're not ready to tell me, there is always tomorrow." And he left, before my Aunt

Lilia arrives from the school which she had been teaching for almost thirty years now. The much-awaited moment in my life had finally eventuated! I'd finished my college degree with flying colours with the attendance of my whole family! After the event, they all kissed and hugged me with so much love and joy! I'd just noticed that the last to greet me was my father. And I didn't ask any question about that! I knew that it was wrong to be resentful to your own father, but I can't help it!

After two years, guess what? Andrew and I had tied our knots in the sacrament of Matrimony and had started our own family. We were blest with three gorgeous, smart and obedient children! God is so good to us that we were both blest with good jobs, myself as a teacher in the local elementary school, and Andrew as an accountant in one of the prestigious companies in town. We had lived in abundance and stability in terms of our daily food, children's education and some other necessities.

Ten years later, Andrew and I took a day off and attended mass on this very special day! It was our tenth wedding anniversary! We sincerely expressed our thanksgiving to God's endless graces and blessings to us and our family. It was at this moment, that I felt some guilt in my heart regarding my parents. Why do I feel this way towards them? Why did they give me up for temporary adoption, until it became permanent? Yes, with my one-on-one with my poor mother, I found out the truth about my father's infidelity and wayward ways. He had one or maybe even more mistresses and also some children from them!

When I was born, being a girl, my own poor mother had lost her complete trust on my father's sanity and decided to give me up for temporary adoption to Aunt Lilia, whom I loved so dearly! I had to admit that it was a shock to me when I'd learned about my father's unfaithfulness and outrageous treatment towards my poor mother! I hated him to death, from then on!

At this present time of my contentment and stable life with Andrew, I'd realised that God always works in mysterious ways! I tried to reverse the episodes that happened in my life, and had contemplated that most likely it would be totally different from what I am today. All of a sudden, the Holy Spirit had touched me and opened my eyes to forgive and forget the darkness of the past and move on in my life! My God, I felt so guilty when I found out the main reason why my mother gave me up for temporary adoption when I was a baby. She had sacrificed her motherhood in exchange for my safety. I felt ungrateful too towards Aunt Lilia, who had given me her absolute love and care! So, with my loud cry, I strongly uttered these words, "Oh, Lord God Almighty, I feel this guilt and stain in my soul, please forgive me, have mercy on me for I am a sinner, I beg you, Oh Lord!" Then, I just felt Andrew's hands on my shoulder with his warm comfort and wiped the tears that kept on flowing down my cheeks as I felt cleansed and healed from all my resentments, hatred and grudges! Oh, thank you Lord God of love and mercy! Amen!

From then on, I was a regular visitor of my poor mother, most especially at that time, her health had suddenly deteriorated due to lung and heart issues. Until one night, I was so devastated to know of her sudden death. After her funeral, my haggard looking father came to me and asked forgiveness for everything he had done and I plainly told him, "Ask forgiveness to my poor mother, not to me!" And I left him with bitterness and pain in my heart! Then, all of a sudden, a woman hugged me and asked forgiveness too! She had introduced herself as Carla, my father's mistress with her daughter Marie! I was shocked and speechless! She gently took my hands and asked for my forgiveness. Again, the same words I'd said to my father came out instantaneously and cried out loud, "Go and ask forgiveness to my mother, so, I could forgive you too!"

God paved the way for our family to move on. Job opportunities came up in the news that Australia needed skilled and qualified workers. When Andrew heard about this, he immediately filled up the application form and underlined the notation "family migration." Being the main applicant, he was called for an interview and had successfully passed it. Then followed by the personal appearance of our whole family. The rest is history!

With our educational qualifications, Andrew and I were so blessed with good paying jobs which had stabilised our finances more than enough to send our three children to Catholic schools and sustain our daily needs and essentials. Time went so fast, until our children had finished their high school and by the following year our eldest will be in college! We felt the hands of God guiding us and providing all our needs!

While we enjoyed the blessings of a comfortable life in this beautiful country, I thought of my father, his mistress Carla and her daughter Marie. I felt that I have to forget my resentments towards them and help them to migrate as well, to enjoy this kind of life. Andrew had totally supported my idea and immediately filled up sponsorship forms for them, including my two brothers. After one week we flew back home and distributed the application forms to my family and fervently prayed for positive results. I surrendered everything to God. Yes, I felt peace and joy when I had decided to sponsor them especially Aunt Carla for that meant a lot to me. Slowly and gently, there is healing and forgiveness happening in my whole being which made me so peaceful and joyful!

My father had the firm decision of not leaving his motherland, but the rest of my family submitted their applications with the help and support of Andrew. After three months, they were all called for interview and later, had received successful results, except for my other brother Jason, who unfortunately had failed the qualification points required. So, Aunt Carla and daughter Marie, my brother Ben, together with his family had left our beloved native land to start a new life in our newly found second home, the beautiful country Australia!

Andrew was deeply touched by my forgiving heart! He can't get over it and uttered these words, "It seemed so impossible for me to do what you had done, Elena! You had completely forgiven your father's mistress Aunt Carla and you even sponsored her and the daughter to be with you here in Australia! It's just too good to be true! I'm so proud of your ever-forgiving heart!"

As what the passage from Luke 1:37 says, "Nothing is impossible with God." Through the power of the Holy Spirit, I had mellowed down and had completely forgiven Aunt Carla. Yes, I had sponsored her and Marie to migrate here in Australia in order to have a better future. And through this virtue of forgiveness, I had also decided to go back home and spend some quality time with my sick father, to find closure in all my questions, and mainly to let him feel too my absolute forgiveness, which I had denied him after my poor mother's funeral. This very emotional mission brought love, peace and joy to both of us and for the very first time in my life, I hugged and kissed my father! It was such a huge release of heavy baggage from the core of my heart, which I had carried for so many years! Two years later, my father peacefully passed away and reunited with my poor mother in their eternal home. May their souls rest in peace. Amen!

Being prayerful and faithful in our daily mass attendance with Andrew in our local church, I found the strength and resilience of emotional struggles in the midst of misunderstandings in the family. My brother Ben was so upset with my refusal to act as a guarantor on a personal loan which he applied in order to set up his own business, in spite of his good paying job! My instant feeling towards his request was fear of the unknown. I remembered one speaker in a spiritual retreat in her words, "Love and money are totally incompatible!" I love my brother, that's why I had sponsored him and his family to be with me in Australia. But his need of my support at this time due to his own personal gain is absolutely unacceptable to me. I thought of my own family, especially of my children's needs. Because of this, he shockingly told me that I've lost a brother and I will never see him again! That hurt me so much! I just prayed and surrendered him to God's protection and guidance.

Days, months and years had quickly passed. One Saturday morning, out of the blue, my sister-in-law Angie called me with her hysterical voice and requested me to visit her husband Ben, who was diagnosed with stage-four lung cancer! I immediately answered positively in order to pacify her. "Yes, I have to see my brother as soon as possible!" I firmly told her.

Ben was already transferred to the palliative care unit of the hospital, which offered specialised medical care for patients with serious illness at the same time give access to the immediate family's non-restrictions on hours and days of visitation. So, in spite of my busyness due to my fulltime work and our family day-to-day activities, Andrew and I, regularly visited him on Saturdays. One afternoon, when we were about to leave, Ben spoke so slowly which I couldn't understand. So, I moved closer to him and saw tears in his eyes and gently said in a very slow and low tone voice, "Elena, my dear sister, I'm truly sorry for I knew that I had deeply hurt your feelings for so many years and yet you had rushed to visit me when I told Angie to inform you about my health condition! Every week, you had never failed to be by my side! I am an ungrateful brother. Please forgive me." I was deeply touched with those beautiful and humble words, I can't control myself, but cry with thanksgiving and praises to our Lord God Almighty for my brother's re-awakening towards our peaceful reconciliation as brother and sister, followed by my sincere words, "Ben, my dear brother, I had always kept you in my prayers in spite of your resentment towards me. I'd offered and surrendered you upon God's loving hands. Yes, I have forgiven you since the day you got upset with me! I love you dear brother!" He bitterly cried so loud with so much guilt in his heart, until he was pacified with my repeated words of sincere forgiveness and love towards him.

After one month, Ben peacefully had gone to his eternal home gloriously reunited with our parents. May his soul rest in peace. Amen!

I thank and praise the Lord for sending me always His Most Holy Spirit for guidance and direction to follow exactly the right path towards forgiveness which leads to my blissful and peaceful life! May God be praised for ever and ever! Amen!

Reflections

What a woman with an ever-forgiving heart! An outstanding and inspirational story about the most difficult and elusive common word to own "forgiveness." It is considered as one of the most precious gems in the treasure chest of one's heart in order to be called a true believer and follower of Jesus Christ. Elena had displayed her ever-forgiving heart likened to the heart of Jesus when He was dying on the cross and uttered the words, "Father, forgive them, for they know not what they do." This was the very first of the seven last words of Jesus!

Let's face it, it's not that easy to forgive anyone who had grievously offended us, because we are just human. But through the power of the Holy Spirit, this can be done. As in Matthew 19:26, "With God everything is possible" absolutely affirms this eternal truth!

Elena was able to forgive her father's infidelity and harsh treatment towards her poor mother. She forgave her father's mistress and even showed her love and concern towards her and daughter! Her brother, whom she had sponsored to Australia with his family had inflicted deep wounds in her heart for disowning her as his sister! This was all because of Ben's obsession with material wealth, and Elena's failure to comply with what he wanted! What an ungrateful and selfish brother to a loving sister!

YES, Elena, a woman with an ever-forgiving heart was able to completely forgive them all through the inspiration and power of the Most Holy Spirit! Amen!

Then Peter asked him, "Lord, how many times must I forgive the offences of my brother? Seven times?" Jesus answered, "No, not seven times, but seventy-seven times."
(Matthew 18:21-22)

Story 13

Bachelor's Life with a Mission

*"I am certain that neither death nor life, neither
angels nor spiritual powers, neither the present
nor the future, nor cosmic powers, neither the
world above nor the world below, nor any creature
whatsoever will be able to separate us from the love
of God, which we have in Jesus Christ our Lord."*
(Romans 8:38-39)

"Martin, welcome to the Seniors' Club!" These
were the words which I had received a million times as texted
messages from my friends, workmates and some of my students
as early as twelve midnight on my feast day! I am officially a
senior as I turned sixty years of age!

I can't help but reminisce the horrendous past, but significant
memories of my life which truly manifested how God's hands
held me close to His heart and saved me from death! I was barely

eight years of age when my parents tragically died in a motor accident. Vividly shown like a thriller movie in my mind, our motorcycle had flown up high as it hit the electrical pole, fatally impacted on my father's head and with that great intensity had landed dead on the ground. While I clearly remembered that I had safely landed on top of my mother's body as she held me so tight around her loving arms, but unfortunately, she fell on a concreted driveway and her head fatally hit the boulder-rocks' edges. They both grievously died instantly! I horribly remembered every bit of that terrible accident which made me an instant orphan! My lamentably non-stop cries had stuck in my mind for so many years! So many cars and other motor vehicles had stopped and tried their very best to help. Then a foreign couple hastily took me! The lady with blonde hair hurriedly wrapped me with a blanket and lovingly held me around her arms like my mother used to do. They swiftly drove me to the nearest hospital, while an ambulance took my parents too just ahead of us. Up to this date, I hate the sound of the siren, because that terrifying sound had traumatised me all through the years!

During the solemn funeral mass of my beloved parents, I was right in front of the hanging cross of Jesus Christ looking at me with all blood around His thorny crowned head! I remembered asking myself at that age, "Why did Jesus die this way? Who could have done such dreadful crime?" I desperately wanted to know the answers! I was so sad after the funeral and started to cry in loneliness, with the fear of my future. Then the foreign couple Patrick and Margaret sat down beside me, tenderly held my hands and said, "Martin, from now on we are your parents and we will look after you!" And they lovingly kissed and hugged me so tight.

Patrick and Margaret were Irish missionaries assigned in our remote village in the early years of 1950s. They had two boys Scott, aged twelve and Jack, aged ten. They looked so intelligent to me because both of them wore eye glasses at that time. I felt so warmly welcomed by them in spite of my dark colour because of my native background. They took my hands and showed me my own room with all the complete furnishings and toys around in case I get lonely. But what struck me was the cross on my bedside table exactly looked alike that hanging cross of Jesus Christ at the church during my parents' funeral mass. I knelt down immediately and prayed to Jesus in my simple words of thanksgiving for giving me an instant family!

My beloved foster parents together with Scott and Jack had gladly shaken my hands as I went out of the university's hall and all said, "Congratulations Martin! We are so proud of you for finally had graduated from University with Bachelor of Science in Psychology!" Then, as one complete happy family we all celebrated over a sumptuous dinner in one of the famous restaurants in town!

What I loved best among the precious gifts that my family had given me was this pendant of a silver plated cross of Jesus with the matching silver chain. I'd worn it straight away and never removed it from my body. I felt so safe and secured when I know that I have the presence of the cross on me. Margaret had teased me since then, that she won't be surprised at all, if one day I would come home as a priest or a monk!

In one of the retreats which the Pastoral Care and Support Organisation had annually given to all the employees, I felt the prodding of the Holy Spirit to continue this mission. So, the next day, I went to see the director and expressed my intention of pursuing further my studies in the Child Welfare and Placement Cases. He gladly agreed and I was sent to our mother company in England for two years. I'd enjoyed my stay there, but suffered a little bit of racial discrimination, which I just totally ignored and rather took it as a challenge. Indeed, I finished my studies and graduated with flying colours!

When I returned back home, I got overwhelmed with so many surprises. Scott was now married with a small baby boy exactly his replica with blue eyes and curly blonde hair. Jack was still single like me. Both my beloved foster parents were still active in their mission, in spite of their age. Fortnightly, they visited the mission area in the remote village where they'd found me more than twenty five years ago. My manager from the Pastoral Care and Support Organisation was also present at home, for he knew very well my details of arrival. He surprisingly had announced his retirement and immediately requested me to apply for the vacant job opportunity! I was deeply honoured with his kind gesture and I did! The rest is history! In the following month I was the manager of our organisation. I was also offered as a professor at the University where I graduated as part time on Tuesday and Thursday nights only. Truly God is great!

Days, months and years had quickly passed. My aging foster parents' health had quickly deteriorated. Patrick's emphysema had worsened, until he was rushed in the hospital for shortness of breath. He had stayed there for more than one week and died in his sleep. Margaret and her two boys were all devastated with the sudden loss of Patrick, but I remained calm and peaceful, for instantaneously I'd felt the big difference between Patrick's peaceful death and my own poor parents' tragic death! I fervently prayed to God for the family's gift of acceptance at this time of loss and grief.

Since the loss of her loving husband Patrick, Margaret had lived a life of solitude. Even I'd organised a trip to the village, she just declined my invitation and said that she felt incomplete without Patrick, which I had totally understood. I felt that she'd lost her active spirit to live and just wanted to follow Patrick. After a year, Margaret had a heart attack. Jack called an ambulance, rushed her in the nearest hospital, but sadly, didn't make it! I had the mixed emotions at that moment! I was peaceful about Margaret's death because I knew how she had longed for her husband's presence and now she had gone to her eternal home and reunited with her beloved husband. I can't help but feel this sadness again of losing both parents. I guess it was my traumatic experience of losing loved ones, but at this time there was deeper trust and faith in the Lord to guide me in the right path towards His plan for me.

Jack finally had settled down and got married. He had managed the ancestral house left by the parents and lived there until they had two children. While Scott was just in another side of town happily married with four children – two boys and two girls. What a lovely and happy family!

You may be asking the question about me! Are you married now or if not, why not and when? Well, I had asked the same questions! During my annual retreat freely given to us by our organisation, I found out my noble calling: To be a bachelor with a mission. Since, Margaret and Patrick died, I filled in the vacancy for a volunteer worker in the village, the poor remote village where they had found me! I volunteered to work there with the permission of my organisation. Fortnightly on Friday morning, I travelled there and stayed for the weekend and back in town on the Sunday afternoon. I felt that something in this place was set for me to do as my main mission. but couldn't identify as yet.

One night, I heard a loud cry of a young girl running, then a sudden silence. I slowly peeped through the curtain and saw her hidden behind the bushy front garden plants. Then I saw the lights of a car approaching, until there was total darkness again! I then quietly opened my front door and gave the young girl a signal to come in, which she hesitantly did. I then offered her food and warm milk which she took as if haven't eaten for a week! This tiny young girl's age of approximately eight years old had suddenly re-opened my tragic rescue by my beloved foster parents, as I had rescued her from the bad people. When she felt at ease, she had innocently told me that the two men were her uncles and often beat her when there is nothing to eat on the table when they arrived home. She bravely escaped from their cruelty and just ran and ran and determined to hide and never see them again! With this sudden and unforeseen sad incident of this young eight years girl named Christina and together with my own tragic experience, I instantaneously felt that God transparently revealed to me the message to rescue and help children in any bad situation, in order to give them a better life, just like when I was rescued by Patrick and Margaret! From there, right away, the mission had clearly and divinely in scripted in my heart and soul for immediate action!

Days, months and years had quickly passed, the mission area had a shelter for orphans and disadvantaged children through our organisation and support from some donors and benefactors. Now that I had turned sixty, everyone in the mission area had gathered around and solemnly lighted candles at dawn and in front of my house sang beautiful songs of praises and ended it with the happy birthday song! I hurriedly ran downstairs to open the door and everyone came in and greeted me with their warm wishes and gave me personalised cards. Then the organiser brought in different cupcakes and the biggest chocolate mud cake I had ever seen and had asked me to blow the candles! After that, everyone was given a piece of cake as a morning breakfast with warm chocolate drinks!

I was deeply touched and so emotional, saying to them, "Yes, I was an orphan at eight years old, but now at sixty, look at my loving BIG FAMILY! I had dedicated my life for the past thirty years in this mission area, which had grown so much in number and added more accommodation as well as the school area. At this place of love, I found a new life and instant loving family and right here, at this place of peace, my blissful life on earth will end!"

I had firmly intended to continue the way I had lived my life, with my absolute belief that God called me to live a bachelor's life with this mission! Being a bachelor, I had never missed out on enjoying life, in fact, I had lived it to the fullest, most meaningful and priceless life. I considered it as my greatest blessing from God! May God be praised forever! Amen!

Reflections

What a brave and strong-willed young orphan boy! Truly, Martin's character is one of a kind! He never looked at himself as being disadvantaged, but rather faced everything he unpleasantly encountered as challenges. In fact, these kinds of encounters made him more resilient towards worst episodes in his life journey. He even regarded himself as the most fortunate boy adopted by the loving Irish missionaries and had shown his endless gratitude towards them until their last breath!

Martin also had loved dearly his two older brothers and had supported them when he had reached the peak of his career with the good paying job! In every little way, he had given them gifts on the occasions of birthdays, anniversaries and Christmas day with no fail!

Through the guidance of the Holy Spirit, Martin had chosen to work in the mission area, just like his foster parents, because this was exactly the place of love and peace which he found. His mission was to give true love to others in particular the children, because he had received this abounding love! What a generous and unselfish mission!

Martin felt the hands of God guiding him all the way through the years and never left him an orphan, but gave him a kind and loving instant family! He definitely became closer to Jesus, as his best friend and counsellor. He fully surrendered and offered his whole life to God's will and plan, which he had rightfully followed all his life and now ready anytime to see his Creator face to face in His Heavenly kingdom! May God be praised forever! Amen!

> *"We know that in everything God works*
> *for the good of those who love him, whom*
> *he has called according to his plan."*
> *(Romans 8:28)*

"To Have and To Hold... in Sickness and in Health"

"Love is patient, kind, without envy. It is not boastful or arrogant. It is not ill-mannered, nor does it seek its own interest. Love is not provoked to anger; keeps no score of offenses. It does not take delight in wrong, but rejoices in truth. Love excuses all things, believes all things, hopes all things, endures all things."

(1 Cor 13:4-7)

Levi and I had successfully celebrated our 40th Wedding Anniversary with a thanksgiving Mass in our local church attended by our immediate family, some relatives and close friends. Levi's wheelchair was parked at the corner side of the church just in case, he felt weak. Throughout the mass, he felt strong and totally forgot on what physical situation he was in at that moment of our renewal of vows! We were both in tears as we lovingly uttered again the marriage vows which we had devotedly uttered forty years ago!

Levi was a very successful real estate agent before we got married. We were both twenty-five years of age at that time when we decided to tie our knots in the sacrament of matrimony. Those were the years of Levi's highest peak in his career. Aside from being an agent, he was also a motivational speaker about real estate business. I was a school teacher and made it easier for me to enrol our two children in the same school where I taught. This was our routine until they had reached high school. Levi spent most of the days and nights during the week on his meetings and functions. But one rule we had in our family: Never work on Sundays! Yes, we made sure that Sunday was spent mainly for God and our family. The kids always looked forward for Sundays, as this was also the time to visit their grandparents on both sides of the family. So, you could imagine how busy we were on Sundays from the early morning after mass till late in the afternoon.

"Bella, did I tell you that I'm the luckiest husband in this entire world?" were the words that Levi had suddenly whispered in my ears, out of the blue! I surprisingly replied with the word, "Why?" Then he told me about his workmate Arthur, who sadly got divorced a month ago. His estranged wife went with the wrong crowd of friends, who were addicted with playing poker machines on Friday nights. This was the issue of Levi's workmate in his divorce application, which later on had final resolution to Arthur's advantage. Being childless, Arthur's wife got bored and lonely in her life and sailed on the opposite direction. She spent so much time with the group of women in the same state of mind and situation. Arthur had convinced his wife to go through counselling but she totally ignored it. Until things went worst and Arthur decided to divorce her.

Now, this is the point of Levi in expressing his sincere appreciation of my dedication to my role as a mother and teacher to our two lovely children and a loving wife! I hurriedly hugged him and responded likewise, to his attributes of being the best provider, a loving father and husband to me! That night was the time of prayers and reflections on God's blessings we'd received for the last twenty years of our married life. Being a real estate agent, Levi was able to secure us a beautiful dwelling and fully paid it off from his own salary and bonuses. My earnings from being a school teacher were enough for our everyday food, amenities and essentials. God is really great in all His blessings and providence to us!

One day, Levi had complained from a severe pain in his upper back and suffered recently from vomiting, excessive tiredness and breathlessness. I was in school at that time, when I got the phone call that he was rushed in the hospital. I hurriedly left school and went to see him. Levi got his presence of mind to call triple zero, when he felt his shortness of breath. He instantly thought of heart stroke. After one week, the doctor went to see us and gave us all the findings. Sadly, Levi's got all the symptoms of acute left kidney failure! I straight away asked the specialist this honest question, "How bad is my husband's left kidney?" The specialist gently said, "Within two months, we will monitor your husband's condition and from there, a decision will be made. The hospital will provide all health care and support possible with the support of a dietician for the right fluid intake and the right diet to follow." So, from then on, Levi stayed home for two months. I advised him to read motivational and inspirational books, as well as watch comedy movies. He followed my advice and every night after our prayers, he shared with me what he read or watched during the day. At this time of pain and sickness, we seemed to be closer and love each other deeper each day. In fact, I had admired his pain tolerance and his positivity towards sickness. He kept on mentioning about the pain of Jesus Christ. "In pain, I share the sufferings of Christ on the cross!" The more I love and honour this man I'd married, and vowed to live with for the rest of my life!

Levi's manager paid him a visit one day and had seriously talked about retirement. He had suggested to use all his sick leave, annual leave, long service leave and finally enjoy his retirement. This is the glorious time to spent more time with God and family. Without any hesitancy, Levi had gladly accepted his kind and practical suggestion.

Not too long from the time that Levi had started his leave, he had received the sad news about his left kidney's failure and for this, it was a necessity to undergo dialysis. Levi and I went to the hospital for more information about the procedure and also had undergone study and training on using the machine. The specialist had recommended the haemodialysis, in which the machine removes blood from the body, filters it through the dialyzer (artificial kidney) and returns the cleaned blood to the body. This 3-to-5-hour process may take place in the hospital or at home three times a week. Once we both get used to it after three months, the hospital will arrange at-home-treatments four to seven times per week for fewer hours each session. Levi may also do haemodialysis at night while asleep, but he preferred to do it awake.

Days, months and years had quickly passed. Levi never lost his lively spirit, in spite of his regular dialysis. He had always looked forward for the weekends, where our two children Jake and John regularly visited their father, with their spouses and two children. Our house becomes so alive on weekends with four grandchildren playing and running around the house. This weekly family gathering certainly made both Levi and myself absolutely delighted! Indeed, such priceless gift from God! After three long years of haemodialysis, the specialist had suggested of kidney transplant! According to him, Levi would live longer with more quality of life. He explained further, that those who had kidney transplant typically live longer than those who stayed on dialysis. Levi just turned sixty years old and the specialist commented that he's still young for a kidney transplant! With this option given, that night Levi and

I fervently prayed for God's guidance to lead us in the right direction. Then, I dreamed of our whole family on a tour and we were so happy to see the Holy Land of Jesus, His sacred places from birth in Bethlehem until His death in Jerusalem! So, I woke up glowing with joy with that beautiful dream! How I wish we can really do that! Being inspired with that dream, I immediately told Levi that I will be his number one kidney donor! He was shocked with my firm decision, and shed tears of joy when I said to him, "Levi, you are my beloved husband and I'd uttered these words in our marriage vows 'to have and to hold… in sickness and in health' remember? Till death do us part! And now is the time to show you how much I love you!"

Nothing can stop me with this decision, as I firmly believed that it was the right direction that God showed me. Being a retired teacher, anytime the hospital can contact me to undergo different test before performing the kidney transplant mainly test on my kidney's health and compatibility test with Levi's kidney. I'd surrendered everything into God's hands and savoured this joy of sharing a part of my body to my dearly beloved husband!

After one full month, Levi and I had received the most awaited news and with deep expectant faith, I knew that everything should be alright. Indeed! all the test results were all positively satisfactory for the kidney transplant, which the hospital had already scheduled within the week. We had requested our own family, relatives and close friends to pray for the success of our 'surgery of love' as what the specialist called it. The rest is history! Praise God!

Today, we had celebrated our 40th Wedding Anniversary with overwhelming happiness and thanksgiving of the gift of love and life! During the blessing of the priest, he said, "Right here, brothers and sisters, we had witnessed an unconditional love like that of God's son Jesus Christ who gave His own life to us all! Likewise, Bella had lovingly offered her own life to her beloved husband!" Everybody had applauded, but with tears of joy and admiration to what had unfolded at that every precious moment! May God be praised forever! Amen!

Reflections

Wow! What an ever faithful and loving wife! Bella had sincerely offered her own life and shared her healthy kidney to her husband's faulty one! Not all spouses are capable to do such sacrificial act of love. It was indeed such a God-like act of unconditional love! In both words and actions, Bella faithfully followed the sacred words of marriage vows which the bride and groom solemnly say to each other on their wedding day. The wedding vows state as:

"I, ____, take you _____, for my lawful wife/husband, to have and to hold from this day forward, for better, for worse, for richer, for poorer, in sickness and in health, until death do us part."

It was Bella's innate loving nature which instinctively pushed her through the guidance of the Holy Spirit to bravely offer her healthy kidney to her beloved husband Levi! What a great virtue to emulate!

Indeed! this inspirational story had showcased one of the greatest love stories ever!

"If I could speak in all the human and angelic tongues, but had no love, I would only be a sounding brass or a clanging cymbal. If I had the gift of prophecy, with no mystery beyond me, no knowledge hidden from me, and if I had faith enough to move mountains, but I had no love, I would be nothing."

(1 Cor 13: 1-2)

Formula: "PPP" Had Cured Me from Cancer

"He sent forth his word and healed them, and rescued them from destruction. Let them thank the Lord for his love, and his wondrous deeds to humankind."
(Psalm 107: 20-21)

The loud crows of roosters serve as the natural alarm to wake up people in our remote village. That's the time for people to push the bamboo poles of their windows to let the sunshine and air in to liven and freshen their small self-built shacks. Such a beautiful and simple life in this tiny village where I'd lived for the last fifty-five years of my life! A sign of another meaningful day! I'd walked every day to town from Monday to Friday for almost twenty minutes towards my office. I'd worked as the local medical centre's clerk for almost thirty years now, which I hadn't even noticed because I'd enjoyed and loved my work.

My loving parents' means of livelihood was fishing and selling fish in the market. I clearly remembered Dad used to go fishing with his group during the day and they go home the next day at dawn bringing with them bountiful catch of fish, ready for the six women, and that includes my Mum to sort and divide them among the six families. Then off they go and sell them in the nearby market. As early as ten o'clock in the morning, mother goes home with a big basket and packages of food, fruits, vegetables and other essentials enough for us family of five for the whole week. Such had been our daily life in this remote fishing village which I loved and wanted to stay the rest of my life. On Sundays, as one happy family, we regularly attended mass and after spent time together in town ending with a picnic in the park! How I'd enjoyed every moment of those precious days! Such a simple life but filled with peace and happiness.

As the saying goes, "Life has got all those twists and turns." As soon as my two brothers had finished their high school, they had left the village and had worked in the city. Then my eldest brother Mark got married after two years and fortunately landed on a good paying job, as well as his wife Irma. But my younger brother Edgar ended up with a wrong crowd of men and got involved with drugs in the city. He got jailed for two years sentence and these bad incidents had broken the hearts of our parents, especially our poor mother! I was the only one left at home, looking after them. I made sure there was cooked food for them, before I leave for work. At night after our dinner, I made sure they're both clean and fresh ready for their bed rest. One time, my mother held my hands so tight and said, "Your father and I are so blest to have such a loving and kind daughter like you! I pray that God will always be with you. We love you so dearly Nelia!"

In the morning, it was unusual that my mother wasn't up as she used to be. Father already had gone for his morning exercise and sunshine walk. So, I went inside their room and held her hands; they were so cold and life less! Oh, my God, my poor mother! Lord God, accept her soul into Your kingdom! She has now gone to her eternal home. May her soul rest in peace, Amen!

Dad was so devastated, as well as my two brothers. I was too, but we have to be strong for Dad! We stayed together for one week to grieve and calm down our dampened spirits. Through prayers and reflections, our sombre spirits had risen up. We have to move on and be back to our daily routines.

After three months, I felt something strange in my body, like a lump under my left armpit. I immediately showed it to my local doctor, who then recommended me to see a specialist. After the biopsy, the specialist straight away told me the sad news of the detection of cancerous nodes. The next step was to remove the cancerous lymph nodes and then followed by radiotherapy. This will kill off any cancer cells that may be left behind after the operation.

This hardest episode in my life just happened so quick and in one split second I had just recuperated from lymph nodes operations. I remembered vividly from my deep sleep that my mother was with me with another woman with a long white veil holding my hands! When I woke up, I knew straight away that my mother and Mother Mary had visited me and watched over me during the whole time. I then prayed the rosary of thanksgiving and straight away felt my healing. During my stay in the hospital, all the nurses and doctors found me so joyful and I even had the time to talk to other patients and motivated them to be joyful and prayerful too. I'd encouraged them to be up at seven o'clock in the morning ready to go for a walk and have a chat and then have our breakfast at the dining hall. Six women regularly had followed my routine for two weeks I had stayed at the hospital.

My father was so happy to see me as a joyful person since I'd arrived home from the hospital. He even commented, "Nelia, I haven't seen you so happy like this! And you looked so refreshed and pretty, as if nothing had happened to you!" Then I replied, "Father, a lot had happened to me. I became doubly prayerful, more positive in my outlook in life and faithful with my doctor's prescriptions!" From then on, I had kept repeating those words I'd learned every time someone asked about my journey. I felt that there was an immediate healing which happened to me, because of God's healing hands.

I had looked forward for my monthly check up in the hospital and all the medical staff were all happy to see my big improvement, especially my specialist. She said, "Nelia, your healing journey had been absolutely amazing!" Always, I would repeat to them what actually I had followed all the way in my journey. I was surprised one day, when the Director of the Cancer Institute invited me to share my healing journey in order to inspire other patients in the hospital. I gladly accepted the invitation with the sincere hope that I would be able to touch and inspire other patients with the same health situation.

When that much awaited moment had transpired, again as if I'd heard my mother and the Blessed Mother Mary's voices with these words, "Go on, Nelia, reveal your secrets!" So, in my speech delivery, I felt God's power within me, fearless and bold, I had proclaimed His healing power with full trust and faith in Lord.

In my final words I said, "With my last check up, the finding was a miracle! There were no traces of cancerous cells anymore! And let me reveal to you the secrets behind this. The formula "PPP" had cured me from cancer! What is PPP? The first P stands for Prayers; the second P stands for Positivity; the third P stands for Prescriptions.

Prayers to our Merciful God is the number one secret. God is our greatest Healer. Let's offer and surrender everything to Him. Believe and have faith that you are healed through fervent prayers and God's healing power!

Positivity in your outlook in life. Look at the bright side of life. When things go wrong, don't go with it. Always look up high in the heavens and soon you will see the sun shining through the clouds! Be joyful all the time, no matter what situation you are in!

Prescriptions. Be obedient and faithful to what the doctors prescribe and instruct you to do. They are blessed by God with their knowledge towards healing the sick and help immensely to the well-being of humankind!

So, my dear brothers and sisters, fellow patients, follow this formula and share lovingly with others! May God be praised forever!"

The huge hall had moved with the loud and long applause and long-standing ovation from the audience! Such a very precious moment, which I will never forget in my entire life! I thank and praise God Almighty for His endless love and mercy!

Reflections

What a powerful woman with absolute faith and trust in the Lord! Nelia's faithfulness towards prayers and obedience on God's will had clearly manifested in her inspiring story. Her cancer episode didn't cause her any doubt at all in her full trust to God's love and mercy. Just like the total faith of Saint Teresa of Avila with her words, "God is full of compassion and never fails those who are afflicted and despised, if they trust in Him alone."

Nelia's simplicity and humility are mainly her virtues which made her so close to God and the Blessed Mother Mary. Her constant prayers had served her intimate communication with God. She was faithful to her special devotions to the Blessed Mother for all her personal and family intentions. These attributes led her to be a vibrant-joyful woman and gained such an incredible positive outlook in life. Her belief in modern science also made her an obedient woman, faithful to the instructions and prescriptions of doctors, for she believed that God also empowered them to be instruments of healing the sick people. All of these, yes, without any doubt made her clean and free from this dreaded disease of cancer!

Indeed! what an inspirational story to be shared to other people with the same health situations and to find encouragement, hope, faith and trust in the Lord's everlasting love and mercy! Amen!

Then Jesus said to her, "Daughter, your faith has saved you; go in peace and be saved from your illness."
(Mark 5:34)

We are God's Gift to Each Other

"For I know the plans I have for you, declares the Lord, plans for peace and not for disaster; plans to give you hope and a future. When you call upon me and come and pray to me, I will listen to you."
(Jeremiah 29:11-12)

I was totally devastated, when I'd learned that my boyfriend for four years was a married man! I felt so sick in my stomach! I cried endlessly and bitterly! When my burst of emotions had passed, I stood up firmly and held my head up high looking up the heavens and said, "Thank you Lord, for leading me to the truth. I will follow the right path to your kingdom!"

In order to easily forget the past memories and move on in my life, I'd decided to move to another remote town in our region. I was able to save money enough to start my small business in buying and selling fish, which had started very well. Due to my loneliness, and away from my family, I found enjoyment in playing cards in clubs. In this particular place, sad memories were totally erased in my mind, and found absolute presence of fun and excitement! The first month of my gambling escapade was an enticement for the amount of money I had won, which of course had encouraged me to come back again and again, and again! After almost two years, I had regarded myself as a hopeless pathological gambler. I had used gambling to escape problems and my feelings of sadness.

This was the worst episode in my life, when I tried to hide from people whom I owed money due to my gambling losses and including the bankruptcy of my small business. I had no way out! My own parents weren't aware of my current financial state, because I didn't want them to be worried about me. Until, I thought of visiting the chapel in our town and there I poured out everything to God all my sins and shortcomings! I cried out the innermost pains and regrets I have and asked God's forgiveness. "Oh, my God Almighty, have mercy on me, a poor and wretched sinner! Have pity on me! Please help me, Oh Lord!"

I got home so tired and went straight to bed, with feelings of relief. For some reason, I felt God's hands comforting me with His words, "Carina, my daughter, rise up and come back to life. I am with you." From then on, I had attended the daily mass before attending to my small business. I had promised people I owed to pay them our agreed amounts regularly. With this commitment, I had worked so hard for longer hours seven days a week! Out of desperation, I also tried my luck in enlisting my name in a pen pal column in one magazine, with the thought of meeting a foreigner who may be able to help me get out of this miserable state! I had asked God's help and mercy about this too!

On the other side of the world, Bryan, a Caucasian man born from an Irish mother and Scottish father had celebrated his 45th birthday in one of the famous clubs in Scotland. It was attended by his parents, and his elder brother Bennett and wife Clair with their cute little boy, some close relatives, friends and few workmates of Bryan. Everyone had enjoyed his birthday celebration, but not so much of the celebrant himself! When he was jokingly asked his birthday wish, he candidly answered, "I wish I could find the right woman for me!"

Bryan had worked so hard as a railway inspector since he was twenty-two years old. He had lived a simple, but busy life: work, home and racing games! During weekends, his passion for racing had made him so occupied, until he'd reached forty-five years old without any girlfriend!

In one occasion of his week-end escapades with friends, one of them gave him a magazine for pen pal writing. He just brushed aside the magazine and totally ignored it. Upon reaching home, he opened his bag to remove all the rubbish, and to his surprise, he saw the magazine again! Out of curiosity, he opened it and saw the pen pal column. Of the five lovely female names written in the magazine, for some reason, he instantly selected the name 'Carina.' He even researched its meaning and found it as "beloved!" He got more excited when he learned that Carina is also a name of a constellation of stars visible in the southern hemisphere! Immediately, Bryan wrote to Carina and mailed the letter as an express post!

Now, back to my own life. My poor parents and whole family shockingly heard about my business failure and gambling addiction. They had suffered in silence with me. So, I pleaded to God for a miracle to happen. I begged Him to help me change my life! That time, I'd completely surrendered my life to God and let Him run my life.

Until that striking moment came, which had changed the alignment of my star in heaven! I had received a letter from a Scottish man named Bryan, who honestly introduced himself and told the story of how he'd decided to write me this letter! As I read the letter, I had imagined his own star in heaven closely aligned to mine! I felt this overwhelming joy and trusting hope, as you could imagine! So, we had exchanged letters for one year. To my surprise on his last letter, Bryan had decided to visit me in my country and even asked the most acclaimed question, "Carina, will you marry me?" You see, within a year of communication, there were no more secrets between us. Both of us had completely opened our lives to each other. So, when he had offered me the proposal, I honestly answered him, "Yes, I will marry you Bryan, if you help me clear my debts!" The rest is history!

My parents and the whole clan did their very best to let Bryan feel comfortable in a totally different environment from where he came from. He had sensibly noticed that and appreciated it, so he simply said to them, "Don't worry about me. I am absolutely fine with everything!"

My parents and siblings had quickly and happily, arranged our wedding, which had officially declared us man and wife. I had to pinch myself, if this was all happening or just a dream! Truly, God showed His mercy upon me and answered my plea! After two months of Bryan's stay in our province, you can see him just like one of us. He had adapted so fast in our way of life.

Until the time had come for leaving my family and native land to start a new life in a foreign land with my beloved husband Bryan! We arrived safely and happily welcomed by Bryan's family. I had settled and naturally adapted the way of life in this beautiful and blessed country of Scotland!

Bryan and I are getting older, and he mentioned about starting to have children, which I totally agreed. Out of his eagerness to have even one child, he even told me the names whether a boy or girl. A year quickly had passed and there was no baby. So, we'd decided to visit the fertility doctor. Another trial had tested my strength of character, when the doctor told me that I was not capable of conceiving a child. We'd tried several medical programs, but all sadly failed. I was so devastated for I thought of Bryan's dream. But I was comforted when he lovingly said, "I married you for what you are and remain in love with you, even we're childless!" Upon hearing those reassuring words, I lovingly kissed and hugged him so tight and said, "I love you more Bryan, that even my own life, wholeheartedly I'll give it to you!"

Being childless, we made ourselves busy. Aside from full time work on week days, we had dedicated our Saturdays on volunteer work in St Vincent's Charities, joined some fundraising events and recently had joined a charismatic group with an evangelistic mission for families. We held our regular prayer meetings and attended teachings, which encouraged us more to be good Christians. The biggest miracle that resulted to our constant fellowship with this group was my prayer for Bryan's positive response to attend the Rites of Christian Initiation of Adults (RCIA) which led to his baptism in the Catholic faith! From day one I had met him, I dreamed of leading him into my same faith, so we can serve God together hand in hand and heart to heart! Praise God for the fruition of my dream!

With Bryan's approval, we had sponsored some of my nieces and nephews in their high school and college education in order to live a stable and dignified life. We had also extended our generous support outside our family when we sponsored two children from the World Vision for their health and education. In the medical world, we were regular blood donors of the Red

Cross organisation in order to help the sick and the dying. Later on, I'd realised that being childless, the more we had the chance to give the best of our time, talent and treasure in every good cause that comes our way for the honour and glory of God!

With my beloved husband, my hero and saviour of my disaster by my side, I couldn't ask for anything more! Bryan kept repeating the beautiful words to me, "Carina, you are God's gift to me. With you, my life became colourful and meaningful!" And always my loving response is, "Likewise, Bryan, you are God's answer to my prayers! So, I can say we are both God's gift to each other!"

Bryan's star in the heavens had aligned with my own star and had joined us together in love, peace, joy and service to God! I thank and praise God forever and ever! Amen!

Reflections

What an inspirational story! Such one of a kind, the simplest, but the sweetest and the most loving of all love stories ever!

I'm so sure that you know all those beautiful quotations about simplicity. To mention a few: "Simplicity is beauty." "Simplicity is the key to brilliance." "Simple things are the best things in life." I don't know who had invented these quotations, but I salute them for putting these beautiful words together which reveal the valid truth of life. I may add the gracious words from Lao Tzu, an ancient Chinese philosopher and writer stating, "I have just three important things to teach: simplicity, patience and compassion. These three are the greatest treasures in life."

Bryan and Carina had just shown simplicity in their own ways, but take a look at the brilliance in their compassion, which had superbly surpassed their passion for a child. They had triumphantly diverted their desire for a child to a higher level of service of love to humanity!

Carina's mission of taking along Bryan into her realm of spirituality had absolutely touched me! This had manifested her great love and gratitude towards Bryan's chivalrous deed of her debt clearance. Carina perfectly knew that together in the same faith and belief, they are always one in service to the Lord!

Both of their virtues of being loving, and caring with total commitment to each other regardless of prevailing circumstances are worthy of emulation! Their simple love story is regarded as one of the most brilliant love stories ever told!

"Trust in the Lord with all your heart; do not rely on your own insight. Let his presence pervade all your ways, and he will make your paths smooth."
(Proverbs 3:5-6)

"The law of the Lord is perfect; it gives life to the soul. The word of the Lord is trustworthy, it gives wisdom to the simple,"
(Psalm 19:7)

A Complete Turn
Around of My Life

"Repent, then, and turn to God so that your sins may be wiped out, and that times of refreshing may come from the Lord, and he may send you the Messiah appointed for you, that is, Jesus."
(Acts 3: 17-19)

It was a bright Sunday morning and for some reason I looked forward for the coming of the prison chaplain, Father Marc and listen to his message. Every Sunday ten o'clock, he visits this prison to celebrate the Sunday mass and explain the Gospel. I knew that I was baptised as a Catholic, for my name is Joseph. But so many bad things had happened in my life. At twenty years of age, I was locked up in jail with a five-year sentence as a drug user and seller.

The last three years was so painful due to some bullying episodes inside the prison grounds. I can't control my anger and used to fight back, which added more discredit to my already existing bad record. My prison counsellor, Sister Anna, a missionary nun kept on telling me to behave inside so that she can help me out. I did try very much, until the last insult was blasted in my ears loudly and maliciously by one inmate, while we were all outside doing our morning exercise. When I heard the tattooed man called me a, "Son of a b….!" I ran to him and punched him so hard till I knocked him down. Then the prison guard came and held me accountable for that! I was punished to stay under the scorching heat of the sun, and deprived me from food the whole day! I truthfully told the incident to Sister Anna, but she said, "I can report this to the Prison Officer, but there will be lots of interrogations. Are you prepared to do that?" Then, I thought about it and said, "No!"

When Father Marc started to read the Sunday's Gospel, I felt so strange in my whole body! I was shaken by the words he read and felt like I wanted to cry out loud! Until he finished the reading and asked everyone to sit. I felt calmer, but my tears kept flowing down my cheeks as if I was cleansed from dirt and rubbish in my body and felt refreshed. The Sunday's Gospel was about repentance from Mark 1:15 which records the inspired summary of Jesus' message as He began His ministry. He said, "The time has come; the kingdom of God is at hand. Change your ways and believe the Good News." Father Marc had explained that to repent means to turn to God and turn away from evil. Repenting is what brings us close to God and ensures our redemption from sin. This explanation had stricken my whole being to the point that I continued crying non-stop! The other inmate had noticed me and gave me the box of tissues which he was holding, as he got emotional too!

After the mass, everyone walked towards the hall for coffee, tea and snacks. Father Marc had approached me and said hello. He had noticed my swollen eyes due to my emotional outburst during the mass. Then, he hugged me so tight and said, "There you go, you can now continue your process of healing, then complete it through your repentance. If you need to talk to me, I will be back tomorrow. I have a meeting with the Prison counsellors." Then, I instantly answered, "Oh yes, Father, I would love to talk to you tomorrow even only for a while! Thank you so much!"

Let me tell you the background of how I ended up in jail, and I was only twenty years old at that time. Just few months before my high school graduation, that particular night was the worst nightmare in my life. I woke up in the middle of the night with the sound of sirens coming from fire rescue trucks passing by our little shanty and all of them were heading towards town. I went out in the street to find out what's going on. I gathered bits and pieces of news that so many buildings and small shops got burned down because of this fire which started from the nightclub building! When I heard the word nightclub, I ran and ran, and ran and called out, "Oh God, save my poor mother, please Lord God, save my poor mother!"

My mother had worked in the nightclub as a waitress and at daytime, as a shop assistant. She got pregnant when she was nineteen. Woefully, my mother's boyfriend left her and said that he will work in the city and come back to marry her. But he never did! I haven't met my father in all my life! Even my poor mother had no idea where he was. A big salute to my poor mother for her firm belief of life's sacredness. She had kept me even she was scared and through her faith and trust in the Lord, she was able to face the big challenge of being a solo parent. To add more pain to her sufferings, she was disowned by her parents! She had no support at all from anybody, but with God's divine providence and loving hands, she had coped with all her struggles. She kept on telling me that, "My little Joseph, all we need in our life is God. God is enough!" So, when I was baptised, she chose the name Joseph with her prayers that I will be like St Joseph with a pure, gentle and loving heart, and never be like my own father!

When I got closer where the nightclub was, I only saw debris, ashes and dead bodies! Horribly, one of the dead bodies was identified as my poor mother! I couldn't accept that tragic loss, so I totally left school and joined the wrong crowd of people in order to fend for myself. I had chosen the easy way termed as "easy money, easy life" - the world of drugs! I felt good after I had one, and another one, and another one! Until

I got addicted. I was nineteen years old, when I got involved in drug-selling and later on landed in jail! I had already served three years of my five-year sentence…

I wasn't able to sleep that Sunday night, because of my guilt and felt myself so dirty. The Sunday's gospel had immensely touched me! I stood up and looked at the cross hanging on the wall and knelt down. Without any word, in complete silence, tears start flowing continuously down my cheeks…. still in silence, but words were in my heart as if I was talking to God heart to heart in total silence! That was an incredible feeling which happened to me for the very first time in my life! I took the cross hanging on the wall, lay down and gently held the cross in my arms as if hugging God! I fell asleep peacefully till morning!

I washed and freshly dressed up ready to meet Father Marc. Surprisingly Sister Anna was with him too! The more I felt this overwhelming joy and peace when I saw both of them, because I believed that God sent them to me as my angels. Surprisingly, they took me inside the Office of the Warden or Superintendent. Father Marc and Sister Anna both recommended that I will be given written test and aptitude test, so I can use any talent I have for the next two years. The Warden had agreed and scheduled it the following week. There will be a team from the Department of Education specialised in determining an individual's skill or propensity. Before Sister Anna left, I asked her if she has a spare rosary and a leaflet of how to pray it. She delightfully gave me her rosary and opened her bag and found a leaflet! I absolutely felt the same or even on a higher intensity when my mother surprisingly handed me my favourite chocolate! So, I hastily said, "Oh, thank you Sister! I love to pray the rosary and talk to Jesus and Mother Mary!" I faithfully prayed the rosary everyday and asked Mother Mary's intercession for the success of my examination and assessment next week. True to Warden's words, the specialised team came and gave me and other eligible prisoners the different kinds of tests which determine our natural inclinations.

After one month, the specialised team from the Department of Education had visited the prison again, to submit the results of our assessments. I truly hoped and prayed to God that something good will come out from my assessment. Help me, my dear God! When they had arrived, the prison guards guided them to the Warden's office. I went to my room and knelt down in front of the hanging cross in silence while holding my rosary. Then after half an hour, there was a knock at my door and I looked at the little square window. I saw Father Marc with the prison guard! I went out and gladly greeted them both, especially Father Marc whom I didn't expect to come at all! Obediently, I followed them wherever they intend to send me with feeling of apprehension. But with the presence of Father Marc, whom I regard as God's messenger, I was fearless!

Surprisingly, they went into the Office of the Warden and asked me to take a seat! Then the Warden started to talk,

"Joseph, you have already served three years, three months and ten days to be exact in your five-year sentence and presently you have a satisfactory behaviour record! With the test results, I gladly announce that you had passed the last remaining year of high school eligibility test. This balance out your fourth year in high school which you had failed to finish. So, you are now officially a high school graduate! Congratulations Joseph!" Everyone applauded in joy and I'd heard Father Marc's the loudest! I was again in tears, but tears of joy and disbelief of what I'd heard! Then, the Warden waited for silence and he continued, "In addition, Joseph, you had passed the exams with flying colours! Your aptitude test was geared towards your talent in arts and drawing. And this is the talent which we, in this prison, in conjunction with the Department of Education will offer you to study. You will be transferred to a rehabilitation centre, where you will continue your college education degree in arts. This centre is within the compound of the University. There are three of you who had passed this aptitude assessment, so the three of you will be escorted by an official prison guard in the premises, until you're given the total release as prisoners!"

Everybody stood up and looked at me with big smile! One by one had congratulated me and given me words of encouragement and warm wishes. In return, I had expressed, "Please accept my sincerest gratitude and appreciation for all the great news that had transpired today, and to all of the people, who had supported me and most of all to our God Almighty who made all these possible! I really looked forward for my transfer next month!"

I still couldn't believe my eyes! This beautifully landscaped garden of roses and all different varieties of flowers with this bright, glorious sunshine and blue skies, is just a perfect picture for a sketch! I readily set my paint stand and small table full of different paint colours and wore my painting coat. That was nine o'clock in the morning and I had finished the final touches of my painting at eleven thirty, ready to be submitted to my art professor. On my way to the professor's office, I heard someone calling my name, behind me. "Oh, Professor Gavin, I was about to see you in your office to submit my painting!" Then, he gladly asked me to quickly show him my painting, which I immediately did! Surprisingly, he said, "I will take it with me right now, so it can be included in the art competition tonight at the University Art Masters' Competition! Do you want to come with me?" I immediately said that I would love to, but I am not allowed due to prison restrictions. He totally understood what I meant and I think he felt sorry about it. So, he left in a rush, in order to make it in time for the final submission!

The following day, on my way to the university campus, I'd noticed students' unusual behaviour towards me, with smile on their faces, which was strange to me. I was already used to the snobbish look from people I'd met along the corridor or even inside the building like library, canteen and classrooms. I totally don't blame them and kept on the words of Sister Anna in my heart and mind: "Joseph, the world is so cruel, just ignore what you hear and see and focus on your goals! One day, you will reap your rewards!" So, this morning, I found it weird and different! People seemed to be kind and friendly to me! Then, all of a sudden, I heard the voice of Professor Gavin and asked me to follow him. He was just such an energetic person; walked so fast with those long legs and I had to sort of run to be side by side with him. We went to the third floor in the Office of the Dean of Arts, Professor Wilson. As the door opened, Professor Gavin gladly introduced me to Professor Wilson and with a big smile he said, "Oh, so this is the grand artist, Joseph! Congratulations, your painting won the most coveted First Place, so you're given the title as the Grand Artist of the Year! I couldn't believe what I'd heard, so I'd looked at Professor Gavin and said, "Yes, indeed Joseph, you did it!" So, I can't help myself, but hug both of them and again had tears in my eyes! I said, "Oh, thank you so much in believing in me! And thank you Oh Lord God Almighty" And they both saw me kissing the rosary's cross!

Days, months and years had passed and I didn't leave the University. After my college graduation, I was instantly offered to teach in the Department of Arts. And guess what? In this university too, I'd met my beautiful and loving wife Jane, who is also a professor in the field of music. We're happily married for one year now and soon, I will be a father! You can just imagine how excited I am to see and lovingly hold my little Joseph, who for sure will absolutely have a pure, kind and gentle father! His father, who once upon a time was lost in the wilderness and darkness of sin, had miraculously experienced a complete turn-around of his life because of God's unconditional love, grace and compassion! Praise to you, Lord God Almighty!

Reflections

Oh, my dear Lord! I can't stop my tears flowing down my cheeks, just like Joseph, who kept crying, in spite of his manliness! This is absolutely such a heart-breaking, but inspiring story!

Joseph was a victim of fated circumstances! It wasn't his fault to be born out of wedlock, not his fault to fall into the trap of desperation, certainly not his fault that wicked people took advantage of his innocence, and had ended up in jail! His traumatic experience of losing his mother, the only person he had in his entire life and at the same time the horrible way he had lost her, were just incomprehensible! No wonder, he ended up in drugs just to forget the trauma and at the same time to have food on the table and money to buy his essentials! He was helpless and hopeless during those turbulent times of his life!

Providentially, Joseph was endowed with his innate thirst for spiritual guidance which had ignited his interest to learn more about God in search of his inner peace. He truly was touched by the word of God on repentance! God is a Merciful God and He sent His messengers through Father Marc and Sister Anna! Amazingly, Joseph had naturally followed all the right path and listened to God's voice in the silence of his heart!

Surely, Joseph was properly raised by his mother as a Catholic as shown in his love and devotion to the Blessed Mother Mary. His mother's firm belief in the sanctity of life, brought Joseph into this world and become a living witness of God's love and providence! His mother's faith and devotion to the Catholic church, made him a devout Catholic too. He became a very prayerful person while in prison and even asked Sister Anna for a rosary and the leaflet which explains how to pray the devotion. From then on, he faithfully prayed the rosary and always asked for her help and intercession as his Heavenly Mother. These traits had definitely contributed to the glory of a complete turn-around of his life through the power of the Holy Spirit! Amen!

> *"God is indeed my salvation;*
> *I will trust in him and not be afraid,*
> *for the Lord God is my strength and my song,*
> *he has become my salvation."*
> *"With joy you will draw water from*
> *the wells of salvation."*
> *(Isaiah 12: 2-3)*

STORY 18

I Saw God's Wonders
in Imperfection

"Sing to the Lord a new song,
for he has done wonders;
his right hand and his holy arm,
have won victory for him."
(Psalm 98:1)

The choir leader had sent me a text message which woke me up with its loud tone. Unfortunately, I had missed to mute my mobile last night! I was forced to stand up and prepare breakfast on an early Saturday morning. I'd checked the time and it was just five o'clock in the morning! I took an early shower and comfortably sat down for coffee and read the text. Oh, our parish priest, Father Andrew requested our choir to sing for his forthcoming 50th Anniversary Ordination as a Priest! What an honour indeed!

Being a retiree at seventy, and a childless widower, I found my happiness and joy in serving our parish church for almost forty years now, since I had migrated to America. My beloved wife, Tanya died ten years ago, from pancreatic cancer. Unfortunately, we were not able to be parents! With me personally, I was a bit scared to have a child for the fear of passing to my child my inborn speech impairment. I had suffered so much from this imperfection during my childhood days. I felt that Tanya might have had the same feeling, because "asking the help of a fertility doctor" was never a topic we had discussed. Surrender to God our innermost desire was our mutual decision. Let go and let God!

I remembered clearly when I was in kindergarten, I used to be traumatised every time my classmates call me, "Thomas, come here and talk to us. Say your name and your parents' name!" Straight away, they will crack up laughing for they knew, it will take forever before I could finish uttering the three names! I was the laughing stock of my class! The more I stutter when I get embarrassed and then I just want to go home. You see, the outside world, full of people, young and old could be so mean and cruel to others especially those with imperfections like me! That's why I became an introvert and a shy person. I used to love and enjoy my own solitude in my own room, fully equipped with so many gadgets which my parents bought for me. My parents ran out of ways and means to improve my speech disorder, because all the strategies had failed and these were officially in the program for my speech therapy. But my poor parents never gave up! With my other two older sisters, we all go to church every Sunday to attend the Holy Mass and every Wednesday to attend The Mother of Perpetual Help Novena. My parents devotedly prayed for her intercession to help me in my speech impediment.

I was scored as average in my intelligence, so I did perform well academically. Because of my speech disorder, oral communication was my weakest point. In writing I used to score perfect grades! So, I still managed to graduate high school with flying colours and was deeply encouraged by my teacher to continue my plan of pursuing the field of Computer Science, for this involves less talking! I was set on what to do with my life, which made my parents so happy and proud!

During that two-month vacation before my college classes, my best friend Carl invited me to join the choir. I looked at him and said stutteringly, "Carl, are you serious? You know that I can't sing!" Then he confidently answered, "I didn't ask you to sing in the choir, but to play the guitar!" I thought of it and I felt a push in my heart to do something good for God this vacation! So, I agreed and asked, "When is the next practice?" From then on, I had looked forward in attending the choir practice and enjoyed my guitar playing, which amazed everyone including our choir leader. He said one time, "Thomas, where have been hiding your talent? Thank God, it came out! You are incredibly the best of our guitarists now!"

Two weeks before the start of my college class, I had practiced playing the guitar alone. Usually, Carl joined me for he's the singer, but this time he was with his parents' anniversary dinner celebration. My practice being alone was a struggle without someone singing, so I tried to sing the lyrics, until I'd finished the whole song! OH, MY GOD! I was able to sing the complete song, without stuttering!

Truly, God is full of wonders! Nobody in my town's medical field can properly explain the reason of how I can sing flawlessly, where in fact I was born with speech disorder! All through the years, I remained as a stutterer. I immediately thought of the passage from the Bible, Luke 1:37, "With God everything is possible."

My parents were so ecstatic, so they went to see our parish priest and asked for a thanksgiving mass as a gratitude for my sudden singing flawlessly! The parish priest gladly agreed and requested the choir to sing in the mass. He specifically asked for me to play the guitar and sing solo the responsorial psalm! At first, my mother had the feeling that he was in doubt about the significant incident, as it was really like a miracle that happened to me. But she brushed aside her negativity and hastily answered, "Oh Father, Thomas would love to!" And with my guitar, I sang gloriously for the Lord God of Wonders! The parishioners' eyes and ears were all focused on me upon singing the psalms on my own, and all in tears of joy and amazement when I had finished!

After four years, I had finished my College Degree in Computer Science and still continued my service in our local church as a choir member. I was employed in a computing company in town and had immensely enjoyed my work. Until, an opportunity came into my life to move to another country. My parents, sister Dolly and I, were sponsored by our eldest sister Gloria to migrate to America. She had migrated there five years ago and married an American. We didn't expect this to happen so quickly and within the year, we had reached our newly found second home. My sister Dolly and I got employed so fast and close to our residence, which was arranged by our loving sister Gloria and her husband, and we enthusiastically started our new life.

After employment, the very first thing my parents and I had checked in the locality was the church. Finally, we found the church close by, which was about half an hour drive! Praise God! From then on, we had regularly attended the Sunday mass, just exactly the same as when we were back home. Then one time, after the mass, I'd approached the priest named Father Walter and asked if the parish has an existing choir. Sadly, he replied, "People are just so busy to sing for the Lord!" His honest answer had hit me so hard to the bone!

After the Sunday mass, I did my best to talk to people and be friendly with the intention of inviting them to form a choir. Then a lady with her younger brother, I guess as they looked alike, came closer to me and said hello. We had a chat and I straight away said that I stutter and to my surprise the lady named Jana just simply said, "Don't worry at all and so does my brother, Jim!" I told Jana about my intention, who surprisingly agreed to join me and my sister Dolly. Through Jana and her brother Jim, I found some answers of how I can sing a song without stuttering, because Jim went through interventions here in America. He told me that according to some specialists, the brain functions differently in singing and distinctively too in talking. You see in singing, the words are generally known by heart, while in talking there is the pressure of searching the words to say. When Jana had explained this to me, I found it very true, as I personally had experienced it!

So, we formed a choir of four people for a start. Every Saturdays, we had practiced at our house for about four songs for the entrance, offertory, communion and closing. After four months, more parishioners had joined us and we formed now a choir of two guitarists and twelve singers! Father Walter was so overwhelmed with joy because more people had attended the Sunday mass compared when we just arrived.

Now you can imagine that I became so busy, due to my full-time work on weekdays and weekend's service for our church! Until some dramatic changes happened in my life! One Sunday mass, straight away, I had noticed a lady wearing a white veil covering half-way her long black hair and with long skirt. That kind of dress style wasn't the usual style worn by women anymore, but I loved it! So, I just said to myself, that the lady could be from another country. After the mass, I was surprised that the lady was outside as if waiting for the choir. And she did, with her brother! They both expressed their interest to join us in singing. That was the start of our friendship.! Yes, her family just arrived from Peru and later on, I had found them very religious and traditional even in their way of dressing. With our regular meetings and communication, I felt that I was in love with Tanya and I openly told my mother about this. She was so happy to hear that and said, "Well, Thomas, it's about time to settle down and give me more grandchildren! I have only one for a long time!"

God is good! Tanya and I had tied our knots in the sacrament of Matrimony! She worked as an administration clerk in an accounting firm in the same building where I worked for six years now. Both of us are nearly on our forties and both waiting for a child to come, but never did. We just left it at that and we kept ourselves occupied in our church service during the weekends. We were such a happy and contented couple who both loved serving the Lord through the choir and in every little way we can.

After ten years of our blissful marriage, Tanya had complained for a severe pain in her stomach. So, I immediately called an ambulance and rushed her in the nearest hospital. She had stayed in the hospital for almost a week for different tests. Then, when the specialist called for me in his office, I felt so nervous. Sadly, he broke the devastating news that Tanya was diagnosed with stage four pancreatic cancer! Then he added more shocking news that she's only given few months to live! Oh NO! Lord God Almighty, help my beloved wife, Tanya! Please save her!

After five months, Tanya had passed away peacefully. Father Walter was able to give her the last rites, which are the sacraments received when the person is nearing death. The sacraments include confession, anointing of the sick and the final reception of the holy communion. I felt so sad about her passing, but felt peace in my heart knowing that she didn't suffer so much and now gone peacefully to her eternal home in the Heavenly Kingdom of God!

You may say that I had lived a sad life, and honestly, I say to you, "You're absolutely wrong!" I had lived absolutely a challenging, exciting, fulfilled and a meaningful life! I couldn't be any happier than what I had achieved in my journey! Since, I had retired, from time to time, I had received letters of invitations from different research foundations to give an inspirational talk to people with speech disorder, which I'd loved to do! It's a simple way of giving back the joy I had experienced having this impediment and share the victory to people. Most of all, I loved to proclaim that I saw God's wonders in imperfection. God himself makes imperfection, perfect because GOD is the

God of Wonders, Power, Might and unconditional Love! May God be praised forever! Amen!

Reflections

What a brave, bold and fearless man of faith! When that magical moment, Thomas had witnessed God's wonders in his own imperfection, everything had changed in his life! He himself became the witness to God's love, compassion and mercy to His people. He was able to overcome his shyness and fear, and bravely went out to invite people to join the church choir. With total confidence and utmost trust in the Lord, he knew that God will surely guide him and will put words in his mouth to express his good invitation to people. God always stayed beside him.

Thomas had also lived a simple, but amazing life! Truly, the glory of God was clearly manifested in his life story as a child born with speech impediment. This was never a deterrent to deprive a person to live a fulfilled life, as shown in this inspiring story of Thomas. Though, he had the short-lived married life with his beloved wife Tanya, both of them lovingly and devotedly shared a full life in their mission. The loss of his precious Tanya didn't stop his mission to proclaim to the world, God's wonders in imperfections. He faithfully continued on his singing and playing the guitar in their local church. God is perfect and has all the wonders, power and might to correct fallibility. Indeed, Thomas is a remarkable person of full faith and trust in the Lord, who personally saw God's wonders in imperfections! May God be praised forever and ever! Amen!

"Recall the wondrous deeds he has done, his miracles, and the judgements from his mouth. O descendants of Israel, his servant, O sons of Jacob, his chosen one, he is the Lord, our God, he rules over all the earth"
(Chronicles 1 16:12-14)

Story 19

My Marriage Had Ended
After Strike Three!

*"Have mercy on me, O God, have mercy, for my
soul takes refuge in you; I will find shelter in the
shadow of your wings, till the disaster has passed by.
I call to God the Most-High, to God who has done
everything for me, and put my oppressors to shame."*
(Psalm 57:1-3)

orn and raised from a military father and a fulltime
mother of twelve children, was not easy for me being the second
eldest in this big family! Mum's voice early in the morning
kept reverberating in my ears, day in and day out, calling out
every morning, "Zoila, check the sandwiches I had prepared
if enough for everyone, and then put them all in their bags!"
Such was our everyday chaotic mornings for three high school
students and four elementary pupils getting ready for school.

Our eldest sister always was in charge of making sure each of us was dressed neatly and properly.

Our father's earning was just enough for our daily needs and essentials. We were very thankful of our father's benefits for our free education from primary to secondary education. When I had reached my fourth-year high school, we had moved to another region due to Dad's transfer of duty. My eldest sister Doris was already working in a big department store as a cashier. She had promised me that she'll be in charge of my tuition fees in college, to my big surprise! Doris wasn't so keen in her studies, unlike me and she knew that very well.

I was so busy with my researches especially with the coming final exams of my third year in college. I took Bachelor of Science in Business Management and aimed at achieving high marks to make my parents proud and my generous sister Doris! True to her words, she had sacrificed herself in supporting me now for three years in my tuition fees. Until one day, she arrived home so sad with haggard look on her face. Mum told her to rest and before bed gave her warm milk. I can't help it, but check on her and find out her condition. To my surprise, she had burst out her emotions and told me that her German boyfriend named Drake is leaving soon because his work contract in the country had finished. He asked her to come with him. She cried and I hugged her and said, "Follow your heart! We are here for you" She was more worried about our father's reactions. I reassured her that Dad will accept this as long as he knows that there is a wedding coming up. With God's grace and blessings, Doris and Drake got married and planned to leave for Germany after two months.

Every one of us had moved on to a new chapter in our lives. I was impelled to stop my studies and worked as a receptionist in a nearby accounting firm, while studying at night even only for few subjects, with my goal to graduate even it took me while. With perseverance and endurance, I finally made it! I followed the footsteps of Doris, so I helped and supported my younger siblings in their studies, until two of them also had finished their college education.

At work, I had met a newly arrived accountant of the firm named Melvin. He was in-charge of the bigtime companies in the city. So, during auditing period, he needed someone to assist him. One auditing season, I was assigned to be his assistant. I found him so prompt, efficient and really professional in his job. We had spent long hours together, especially when there were so many issues he had to review. One time, it was already seven thirty at night and we were both surprised how late it was. So, he invited me for dinner which I gladly accepted! That was the start of our close relationship and had blossomed into a beautiful love for each other. He had proposed to marry me and I gladly accepted!

Days, months and years had quickly passed and God blest us with three gorgeous children! Melvin seemed to be more ambitious to have a better life style for his family. At work, family migration was the number one topic, especially when one accountant had already left with his family two months ago. And because of this, Melvin had thought of it too. He enthusiastically applied as well and we just surrendered everything in God's loving hands our family's brighter future.

God is good! After two years, we had left our native motherland and migrated to Canada. We had settled in Vancouver and providentially we felt the warm welcome of the friendly neighbourhood, who were mostly migrants like us. We also joined the Catholic Charismatic group and became active parishioners in our local church. Melvin and I both landed with good paying jobs enough to maintain our daily needs and education of our children. Everything ran smoothly in every aspect of our lives!

Another dramatic change had transpired in our journey. Melvin was offered a high paying job by his mother company in Toronto! My sudden reaction to this was more of apprehension than appreciation for I know the ripple effects of moving again in different angles particularly our children's school, friends and environment. I have to leave my work too which I had loved! But we have to move with him to be a complete family! With God's blessings, again, we had settled easily in this new suburb which was more city like than our former neighbourhood. All of us was able to adapt to the new environment, and contentedly had moved on.

My mother kept on saying, "My daughter, life is not always a bed of roses, but also of thorns!" So, my life with thorns had started, when I had noticed something strange on Melvin's actions and moods. He was always quiet and busy in the study room on his computer. One time, out of my curiosity, I had opened his drawer and shockingly saw an unfinished letter to a woman. Upon his arrival, I had confronted him and showed him the letter. He was caught flatfooted! No way out! So, he just asked forgiveness and said, "Zoila, there was nothing serious about it. I'm so sorry." I was cheated and terribly hurt with that, but forgave him for the sake of our children. We had moved on from there, but I felt that our relationship became so cold and had lost my trust in him.

You see, Melvin's work contract involved overseas trainings and conferences. So, twice in a year, he was away for almost two months. After two years, I had found out that during his overseas work related trips, he passed by Vancouver for two days of stay before going home to us! I had investigated this and devastatingly unfolded again his infidelity. There was a third party! What did I do? I had forgiven him again for the sake of our family!

I really did my best to keep our marriage intact. At work, I was given a redundancy pay and shared him certain amount of that money to pay his credit cards and some liabilities. In spite of his unfaithfulness, I still showed my care and respect, with the hope that he would be touched by my genuine generosity and would remain faithful to me.

Remember this passage from Matthew 18:21-22? "But how many times can we forgive our enemies? Seven times?" Peter asked his Master. Then Jesus replied, "No, seventy-seven times!" Honestly, I had tried to follow that, but this time, my own children had pushed me to separate from their wayward father. They said, "Mum, you had enough! You deserve to be happy!"

You see, he cheated again for the third time! One of our children saw Melvin with another woman in a restaurant so close to each other like young lovers! Of course, our son had reported this to me, which at this point my anger and frustration towards his infidelity had reached its peak! My forgiving heart had turned into a heart of stone! Forgive me, Oh Lord my God! You are a Merciful God, have pity on me! We had parted ways immediately and I had officially filed our divorce after two years!

At this present time, I live a very simple, but blissful life of a divorced woman with seven gorgeous grandchildren. I joined our community's projects on charitable works and faithfully served our local parish in the church choir. On weekends, my three children with their spouses and children regularly paid me their visits on rostered basis. On special occasions like Christmas, Easter, anniversaries and birthdays, they organised really nice venues for the celebrations or even weekend getaways and just pick me up. During these occasions, I'd asked the children to invite their father regardless of our marital status, just to show him that this family still care and recognise him, but he never did accept any of the invitations. Deep inside me there is peace every time I'd requested the children to do that act of kindness towards their father, though with no success. I just still hope and pray that one day, he would join us even only on special occasions especially on Christmas day.

All through the years, I had always looked forward for the children's surprises of beautiful and impressive places with great ambience and delicious flavoursome food! Every time I had expressed my great impressions on their choices, they all proudly say, "Mum, you absolutely deserve the best!" With those sweet words, I exactly knew what they all meant! Thank you, Lord God for giving me such loving family! Praise you, Oh Lord God Almighty! Amen!

Reflections

What a remarkable woman of Christian faith! Zoila did her best to be a real follower of Jesus Christ in this virtue of being forgiving to one's enemies. But her limits had reached its peak! Yes, she believed that God is a merciful God, who will surely understand her for being unforgiving due to her husband's unfaithfulness. She had asked God forgiveness towards her unforgiving heart and filed a divorce against her husband.

At this point, just reflect on Zoila's decision! Would our decision be the same like Zoila's resolution? Or would it be the opposite, just like, go on with life and accept Melvin for what he is? Be a martyr in order to keep your family intact? Would you be able to tolerate Melvin's infidelity? Or perhaps, consult a marriage counsellor before filing your divorce? Well, this could be all treated as case-to-case basis.

In Zoila's case, the word "trust" completely was erased from her heart, because she had known deeply well her husband's calibre in women, which she wasn't able to tolerate. Even their own children had absolutely disapproved of their father's wayward ways.

But what strikingly notable on Zoila's character was her innate soft-hearted nature of still hoping and praying that one day, even for a while Melvin accepts their invitation to join the family for a meal and meet the grandchildren. She had constantly asked her children to keep inviting Melvin till one day, he answers positively! To me, she had shown traces of forgiveness after years of separation and her Christian values had won over hatred and resentments! With that act of humility, I'm absolutely sure that her children and grandchildren will surely remember this virtue in their lives and follow the good examples she had encountered in her journey. What a remarkable Christian woman worthy of emulation! Praise God Almighty!

"Bless the Lord, my soul; all my inmost being, bless his holy name! Bless the Lord, my soul, and do not forget all his kindness. He forgives all my sins, and heals all my sickness; he redeems my life from destruction, and crowns me with love and compassion."
(Psalm 103:1-4)

There is Joy and Glory in Pains and Sufferings

"If we are children, we are heirs, too. Ours will be the inheritance of God and we will share it with Christ; for if we now suffer with him, we will also share in his glory. I consider that the suffering of our present life cannot be compared with the glory that is to be destined to be revealed to us."

(Romans 8:17-18)

"Oh my God! I am truly grateful of all my pains and sufferings!" These are the beautiful words I constantly say at the end of my daily prayers. You may be wondering and asking this question, "What made her so thankful about sufferings?" Well, allow me to tell you my life's journey.

At the height of my career as an accountant in one of the prestigious firms in the city, this terrible accident happened which had dramatically changed my outlook and priorities in life. I am a mother of three children and happily married for twenty-five years. At work, I was always the last to leave and made sure, I had turned off all the lights and turned on the alarm system. With all the hustle and bustle in the city, I'd walked so fast in order to catch my bus and wanted to be home early in order to prepare our dinner. I hurriedly crossed the road, when I suddenly heard a piercing noise of car brakes' screeches and then a thunderous car crash! I instantaneously felt that I was hit and I was! It was so sudden! With just a flick of one's finger, people had gathered to check my condition! A very brave lady dressed in white, whom I readily knew was from the medical field, had readily checked my pulse and told me not to move and keep still. She saw my name on my ID clipped on my blouse and said, "Paulette, you will be alright and just hang on. God is with you!" Until I'd heard the sound of the ambulance siren.

That time of my accident was the craze of the newly invented mobile phones, where almost every adult person would have one! I just couldn't believe later on how the news can spread like fire through these mobile phones. When my family had received the shocking news about my accident, they'd immediately made use of their new communicative device to request prayers for me addressed to all relatives, friends and our community prayer group. I was amazed when I found out of how many people had sent me messages, cards, flowers within such short period of time. I felt the pouring of prayers and love from everyone who had heard about my accident and some people whom I didn't even know! This was the catalyst which had changed my spirituality, outlook, attitudes and priorities in life.

I clearly remembered when I was at the emergency room, when doctors and nurses were so busy doing the different tests, x-rays, and CT scans, I just offered myself to God's mercy and instantly took the opportunity to ask forgiveness for all my sins and as well as forgave all the people who had offended me. I was ready to die and see God face to face! This was the point when I had offered my severe pain to Jesus as my share with HIS pain and suffering while dying on the cross. I vividly remembered too, a priest was beside me and gave me the sacrament of the anointing of the sick, which I was so thankful and felt instantly my physical healing! I was in tears when the priest gently spoke to me and affirmed my healing, "Paulette, receive the healing of our Almighty God, the Greatest Healer, believe and have faith in Him!"

Miraculously, after all the findings of fractures in my hip, a couple of ribs and some cuts in my head, indeed, not a single operation was required! Instead, I would have to be on complete bed rest for six weeks! The medical term "complete bed rest" meant that I was not allowed out of bed at all, therefore I had to do everything in bed. I'd stayed in the hospital for five long weeks, but it was such a big blessing for me! You may ask why? This was the time when I had all the precious time with God in prayers and just in silence with Him, heart to heart with Him! It was the time that I'd the opportunity to read the books which were just kept aside gathering dust. This was the time when I felt loved by my family, relatives, friends, workmates and community prayer groups every time they'd paid me visits, or sent messages, flowers and cards. My hospital stay was indeed like a holiday with the Lord! I was released just in time for Christmas. It was such a big relief and a big blessing to be home even though in a wheel-chair. God is good!

During my recuperation, all of a sudden, I'd felt a heavy pain on my chest, so my husband rushed me to the hospital. The doctors found out that I'd a mild heart attack which was caused by three blocked arteries. Again, through prayers, I was spared from heart surgery, instead the cardiologist gave me medications with caution to watch my diet and blood pressure.

This was the beginning of a change of lifestyle: a disciplined life on my prayer life, family togetherness, healthy eating habits, and community involvement. I became not only doubly prayerful, but triply and reaped the reward of profound closeness to God and the Blessed Mother Mary. I had learned to ignore petty issues, instead I made the most of everything at any given time and opportunity. For me, every day was a blessing; a bonus of a new life. So, I'd made sure that each day I had spent was my best. As the saying goes, "Live each day, as if it was your last." I'd used this saying as my mantra, from then on.

Our three children had successfully finished their college education and landed on good paying jobs. It was time for me and my husband to retire and fully give our time for the Lord in service. Before retirement, I had already planned what to do, like teaching Scriptures to the children in public schools, in order to know God, love Him and serve Him even in small ways. I thought of being a volunteer to help in food preparation for the "Meals on Wheels," a project of St Vincent de Paul. My heart was set on these two major goals. In addition, I had also committed to continue my liturgical services in our local parish church. So, upon my retirement, indeed, I was able to execute my goals which gave me a fulfilled and peaceful life.

I thought, my life would revolve on those projects which I had lovingly and joyfully joined. Until, another big challenge had transpired in my life. You see, I knew that one day, I will wake up with a problem in my kidneys. I was born genetically with polycystic kidneys, an inherited disorder in which clusters of cysts develop in the kidney. According to statistics, many people with this condition will have kidney failure by age 60. So, during my retirement, I started to feel the pain in my urinary tracts, back and side pain and high blood pressure. It was time for me to have a dedicated kidney specialist to monitor my condition. Again, I offered my pain to Jesus as my share with His suffering while dying on the cross. Every time I gave my loving offering to Him, I seemed to feel numb in my whole body! There was no pain at all!

My kidney failure became worst to the point that I desperately needed dialysis. Through all the different tests and studies conducted by my kidney specialist, finally he had reached to a resolution that I have to undergo the peritoneal dialysis. According to him, it is a type of dialysis which uses the peritoneum in a person's abdomen as the membrane through which fluid and dissolved substances are exchanged with the blood. It is used to take out excess fluid, correct electrolyte problems, and get rid of toxins. So, I had no option but to follow the best solution to help me survive this fatal disease. I was immediately enlisted for the necessary procedures and trainings on how to use the machine, as well as take extra good care for its proper cleanliness and hygiene. This process is done three, four or five times in a 24-hour period while awake during normal activities. Each exchange takes about 30 to 40 minutes. When I got used to this regimen, I felt comfortable doing it mealtimes and at bedtime. These particular times become my prayer times and reading books about saints and spiritual reflections.

I totally offered and surrendered my life in God's hands, for I have no idea until when will I be doing this. In every pain and suffering I had encountered, I prayed to Jesus and say, "With my pain, Lord Jesus, let me share with your pain while dying on the cross for our salvation." Then always, I felt this indescribable joy and glory in my heart! Amen!

Reflections

What a strong, persevering and resilient woman of faith! People like Paulette are hard to find, especially nowadays, where people tend to follow the line of least resistance, easy and painless surgeries, and even, unbelievably the modern painless birth! People seemed to be afraid to suffer and be in pain, as they tend to resort in pain killer drugs until the body gets addicted to them.

Paulette had her special way of pain tolerance and that is her special way of offering the pain and suffering as a way of sharing them with the pain of Jesus while dying on the cross! Indeed, this requires a deep and close relationship with God in order to understand that feeling of sharing the pain. It did truly work in her ways, and no wonder she constantly feels this joy and glory, every time she encountered pain in her body. Paulette firmly believes that when she is suffering, God is right beside her!

2 Corinthians 1:5, "Just as the sufferings of Christ overflows to us, so through Christ our comfort overflows." This explains why Paulette offers and shares her pains and sufferings to Christ's sufferings, for in doing this, profoundly gives her comfort. This comfort refers to strengthening and deepening of her faith and trust in the Lord and in turn she experiences immense joy and glory! No wonder, whatever she faces in life, she's strong and resilient, as well as persevering despite difficulties and failures.

What an inspiring story of strength and deep faith in the Lord; a remarkable story of resilience and endurance in pain and sufferings transposed into joy and glory, which can only be made possible through the power of the Holy Spirit! Amen!

"Instead, you should be glad
to share in the sufferings of Christ
because, on the day his glory is revealed,
you will also fully rejoice."
(1 Peter 4:13)

I Finally Found My Eternal Vocation

"For I know what plans I have for you,
declares the Lord, plans for peace and not for
disaster, plans to give you hope and a future.
When you call upon me and come and
pray to me, I will listen to you.
When you seek me, you will find me,
and when you search for me with all your heart,
I will let you find me, declares the Lord."
(Jeremiah 29: 11-14)

"Praise God for all the blessings and constant protection to my family!" These are my regular prayers kept repeated in all the scheduled Divine Office Prayers from morning till night in this semi-contemplative convent where I have been assigned for almost twelve years now! Yes, I am a mother of three children and a grandmother of five gorgeous grandkids and currently a missionary nun! Right now, you may be asking the question, "How could that be possible?" I can straightforward give you my answer, through the scripture passage from Luke 1:37 which states, "With God nothing is impossible."

When I was twenty-nine, I married Noel, my childhood friend, high school sweetheart and son of a farmer who owned hectares of rice fields and also sugar plantations in our province. But he never stayed and worked in the farm due to his health condition. He had been a sickly young boy since childhood, but had shown great strength in talking and inspiring people through his good communication skills and charm. So, he became a teacher like me, but he taught secondary education, while I taught the primary level in the same school. We were happily married and blessed with two children: a three-year-old gorgeous girl and one-year old cute boy. Until, one day he fainted in school and was rushed in the hospital. He was so devastated when he found out that he had this fatal heart rheumatism and unable to work! So, this made me contemplate to work overseas in order to earn more money to fend for my family and sustain all our daily needs including the medical expenses of Noel.

After a month, I had received a job acceptance as a babysitter of two children of a couple who were both busy engaged in business, which involves traveling for two to three months away from their children. It took them a while to decide the qualified applicant. "Cristina, congratulations for getting the job and you'll be leaving as soon as possible!" I was over the moon, when I had received this urgent message from the recruitment agency which had dramatically changed my life! But deep in my heart, I felt sadness for I will leave my children and Noel under the care of my parents.

A month later, I was the babysitter of these two lovely girls, same age as my own children! I took care of them and loved them as if they were my own! My employers were so happy with my diligence and initiative in doing other household chores aside from looking after the kids and had gained their trust in me. They had given me their whole year travel schedule and it showed that in two months' time they will be away.

One morning, I felt so sick, weak, dizzy and could hardly stand up. My lady employer saw me in this condition and called home health service. A doctor came, checked my blood pressure, took my blood test and urine test too. The following day, I had received a shocking news that I was pregnant for my third child! Immediately, I went to my room, knelt in front of the altar and prayed for wisdom! I felt lost and didn't know what to do. Then, I heard a knock at my door and my lady employer said, "Don't worry Cristina. Stay until your eight months pregnancy and then you may go home to give birth in your own country. I would like you to be back when you're ready." I was so happy and peaceful with that unexpected kind arrangement from my employer.

I gave birth to a baby boy, who exactly looked like Noel, so we had christened him with the name Noelito. I felt total sadness again for leaving my family especially my newborn baby, but I had no choice. Noel's health situation had worsened and this aggravated the heaviness in my heart as I left that gloomiest day of my life. That was the last time I saw Noel, because after two months, he sadly passed away!

Days, months and years had passed, and my children had reached their secondary education and same as my kind employer's children, which made me think that they might not need me anymore. I was right! After a month, they gave me two months' notice of job termination, but generously gave me a referral letter for another employment. They had advised me to immediately apply for it, which I readily did before I left them for my most awaited reunion with my three children in my native land.

Through God's blessings, graces and providence, I was accepted as a caregiver to a paralysed old man in Italy. With heavy heart, I left again my three children under the care of my parents. I had met an eighty-year-old immobile man Giorgio, who lost his wife due to cancer three years ago. Later on, I found him as the kindest person with a purest heart that I'd ever met in my life! After a year, I was shocked when he offered his help to sponsor my three children to migrate in Italy, through marriage! I gladly accepted that kind arrangement for the sake of my children's better future. After one year, we became a complete family! My three children had all finished their university degrees and were all stable in their good paying jobs. I couldn't ask for anything anymore from God because of the smooth sailing of our lives! Giorgio had treated my children as if they were his own, like the loving way I had dealt with my previous employers' children! As a family, we thanked Giorgio for his divine presence in our lives! We all believed that he was God's messenger to show His great love to us! Until one morning, we felt so shocked and devastated, when we found out that Giorgio had passed away in his sleep. We had grieved and mourned for the loss of our hero, an old invalid man with the unselfish, purest, and kindest golden heart!

My three children were all blissfully married and happily settled in their own abodes. This was the period in my life when I felt something was missing. In spite of my joy and contentment with our present status in life, especially my children's accomplishments, I felt that there was a vacuum or an empty space in my heart.

Until one Sunday mass, there was an invitation for a weekend retreat regarding an interesting topic: The Real Meaning and Purpose of Life. Instantaneously, my heart leapt with joy and enthusiasm to attend it. That unforgettable weekend was indeed the catalyst for a drastic change in my life. I heard God's call for me to fully serve him and mysteriously found the missing piece to fill in the empty space in my heart! With so much peace and joy, I had immediately consulted my children in my resolution to join a religious order and be a nun for the rest of my life! To my great surprise, they were all happy in my decision and simply said, "Our ever-dearest mother, you had worked so hard all your life and you deserve to be happy! And who wouldn't be happy to be with God for eternity? We love you dearest mother and delighted to join you in your happiness!" We all hugged and kissed each other with tears flowing down our cheeks, full of joy, peace and great love! Deep inside my heart and soul, I quietly talked to God and said, "Yes, Lord I finally found my eternal vocation! Help me to be your deserving and humble servant! Thank you, Oh Lord God Almighty! Amen!

Reflections

Wow! What "a one of a kind" heart-warming story! My tears kept on flowing down my cheeks too! Cristina's steadfastness and firmness in all the different challenges that had transpired in her life, truly manifested the presence of God's guidance and providence in her entire life. This was because she never lost her strong connection with God's loving hands. She had clung and sought God's mercy, especially during those harsh and painful times which kept her strong and resilient. Because of her deeper relationship with Jesus and the Blessed Mother Mary she had endured all the trials she had encountered with strong faith which she was fully gifted with.

Through God's love and mercy, Cristina met all the good and loving people like her kind employers, who totally understood her situation and had helped her to move on in her life. They had gratefully shown their deep appreciation towards her utmost dedication and love in her role as babysitter to their children, by the referral letter they had lovingly given her, which significantly helped her family in the end! Giorgio was regarded as their hero. Yes, I absolutely agree that he was their family's hero! Giorgio was an angel sent by God to them!

Through prayers and invocation of the power of the Holy Spirit, finally Cristina found her missing piece in order to fulfill the real purpose in her life! With the remaining years of her life, she had finally found her eternal vocation to serve God fully as a religious missionary nun until the end of her life's journey here on earth! Praise God! Amen!

"Make known to me your ways, O Lord;
teach me your paths.
Guide me in your truth and teach me,
for you are my God, my saviour;
I hope in you all day long."
"Those who fear the Lord will learn
from him the way to choose."
(Psalm 25: 4-5, 12)

Story 22

The Philanthropic Power Couple

The word of the Lord came to me saying:
"Before I formed you in the womb I knew you,
before you were born, I set you apart,
and I appointed you a prophet of the nations."
(Jeremiah 1: 4-5)

Margaret was awarded as the "Miss Charity Princess of 1939" which was the first joined project of our town's municipality and local school for a noble cause. It was a remarkable event which had dramatically changed her life. She was a teacher of the town's secondary school and was selected as one of the candidates to run for the title for a good purpose. Money raised for this competition will be used for funding the education of the disadvantaged families. Those poor students who can't afford to pay their tuition fees will be benefited in this project. There were fifteen semi-finalists, when the judges had trimmed them down to three finalists. Not even in her wildest dreams that her name would be called as one of the finalists, let alone be declared as the WINNER! She wasn't able to control her tears of joy, as the Town Mayor had gently put on the sparkling crown on her head and a young gentleman handed her a bouquet of white and red beautiful fragrant roses! The crowd had thunderously applauded her final and brief acknowledgement to all those, who had supported her in this noble endeavour!

Coming from a poor family herself, Margaret knew the hardships and struggles of poor parents to send their children to school. Much to their desire to get their children educated, they found themselves helpless because they had no means to pay the tuition fees. The government only funded the primary education, but not the secondary one. So, when Margaret became a teacher, she felt so sorry for the poor children. This motivated her to exert all her efforts to contribute to this cause, through hard work and perseverance in door knocking for donations, asking rich people's support and writing letters to well-known philanthropists of the town as well as the neighbouring towns. She was able to raise the highest amount of money which was far beyond her expectations! Finally, Margaret had reaped the glorious award and title as the queen of charity for that memorable year! That was the beginning of her mission of supporting the disadvantaged families in education through donations and pledges from the rich and famous!

Marco is my name, seventy-eight years old and I am on the last chapter or sunset of my life. Let me share this very inspiring story, because I was one of the fortunate poor students, benefited from that noble cause in 1939. Because of that initial and remarkable mission, I had finished my secondary education free from tuition fees. In order to qualify in this free education, the applicant must have one major criteria of excellence of academic grades not lower than 85 per cent in all subjects. He undergoes some aptitude and ability tests in order to see how and where he can help in the schools' numerous jobs. I was assigned in some administrative and clerical jobs in the office. When the applicant successfully passed the criteria and identified his abilities, he's regarded as working student and at the same time a scholar. Being a working student is a productive way of giving back the school's generosity of being a recipient of a scholarship. It's a give and take process.

Let me continue the story of Margaret, whom I had immensely admired in my entire life. Aside from her outward angelic beauty, inside she had a pure and genuine heart filled with compassion. When I had finished my high school, Margaret was already married to a well-known lawyer in town named Attorney Roman, a son of an affluent landlord with hectares of farmlands planted with rice, sugar cane and other seasonal crops. From that year 1939 she was reigned as the first princess of charity, the fund-raising program had continued on every two years, until funds for the noble cause kept growing and growing. I firmly believed that God once again had worked in His mysterious ways, when the famous lawyer Attorney Roman was involved in the formulation of laws, rules, policies and other legal documents required for the possible expansion of the humble secondary school into college in the future. Later on, Madam Margaret became the principal of the school.

Soon after World War II had ended in 1945, the secondary school became a college which had offered levels of education from primary, secondary, until tertiary education. Through the noble ideas of the Board of Trustees, with the major role played by Attorney Roman as the legal adviser and one of the primary stockholders, the college had achieved its highest ideals through education. The College had offered some selected college degrees like Bachelor of Science in Liberal Arts, Elementary Education, Education and Commerce. That was the start of a big boom of higher degree of literacy in our small quaint town. It was well known for its quietness, lack of energy and passiveness due to the inadequacies of families to send their children to school for the next level. Money for the tuition fees was the biggest hurdle for most of them. The opening of this college had brightened up the spirits of the people, especially when they had learned about the college's offer for scholarships.

Again, with God's grace and blessing, my own family had benefited from the scholarship program offered generously by the college. I clearly remembered that day when Madam Margaret had called us for family interview. My wife Luisa and

I were so nervous and fervently prayed for a successful interview. Being the high school principal, Madam Margaret was the very first person whom the applicant will meet together with the parents and the most important document: the student's report card. Right after the interview with the parents and child, traditionally, Madam Margaret never failed to ask the student to stay for 'briefing' as she called it. At that particular moment, when she had requested our daughter Laura to stay, I was a little bit anxious as to what questions she would ask her. So, I just prayed to God for good outcome, because our general interview went well especially with Laura's excellent grades in her report card!

While waiting for our daughter to come out from the principal's office, my wife Luisa and I had suddenly felt sorry for Madam Margaret and Attorney Roman for being childless. They were not blest even with only one child! We even said that they could adopt if they wanted to, but they never did! Our conversation had stopped, when not too long our daughter Laura happily came out from the office!

That night, during our dinner, I had the chance to ask our daughter Laura as to what questions Madam Margaret had asked her or what topic they had discussed. Laura felt my eagerness to know, so she didn't want to disappoint me. She had emotionally disclosed to all of us, her fifteen-minute blissful stay with the "Mother of the Poor" as she had called her. These were the inspiring words of Madam Margaret,

"Don't despair if you are poor, because you are loved by God! When you are poor you know God. There are some people who are rich, but don't know God and don't love God. This is the main reason, why I wanted to talk to you. You had passed all the requirements to be a scholar! Congratulations Laura! From now on, be happy that you are a poor girl. As Jesus said in His Sermon on the Mount, Luke 6:20, "How blessed are you who are poor, for the Kingdom of God is yours." Study well, aim at your goal and live a good life, and never ever forget God who loves you unconditionally. You are allowed to be rich, but remain in love with God. If you become rich, help the poor. Live a meaningful life to the fullest, my dear daughter! You make your own life with God's guidance. Together with my dear husband Roman, you are now one of our daughters in our hearts! God bless you forever!"

Laura had finished her short disclosure with tears kept flowing down her cheeks and all of us too! So, we all stood up, hugged and kissed each other with love, peace and joy in our hearts!

After our family prayers, I had contemplated on Madam Margaret and Attorney Roman's life. I was deeply touched by Laura's revelation of the mini homily of Madam Margaret! Oh, my God! I shouldn't feel so sorry for them, but rather lift them up to the heavens for their noble deeds and rejoice! They were both God's messengers to help the poor people's education in order to live a better life! I myself, had finished high school education through those funds raised during Madam Margaret's charity work. And now, as a father, my own daughter Laura had also benefited from the college scholarship program through the noble ideas of the College Board of Trustees, headed by Attorney Roman and support of Madam Margaret. Through this remarkable philanthropic power couple, though childless of their own, had tremendously fostered not only hundreds, but thousands of poor boys and girls to live a better life, with deep love for God. All of them had learned so much from the fifteen-minute teaching of the "Mother of the Poor" and as a couple, I personally call them "Foster Parents of the Poor." Truly, their union in marriage as a childless couple was God's plan for them to achieve the highest level of parenthood! God called them for a noble mission as the philanthropic power couple to lift up the dignity of the disadvantaged children through education, with strong faith and trust in the Lord! Praise God for this notable couple, who had left a treasured legacy to mankind for the advancement of the future generation! Amen!

Reflections

What an inspirational, motivational and incredibly remarkable life story! How many philanthropic power couples are there in the whole planet? How many Margarets and Romans are there in this world? If only there are more people like them, our world would be a better place to live in! We can imagine a finer society, peaceful living, cleaner environment, and higher standard way of life. These scenarios are the effects of having more affluent people, with dedication to philanthropic and altruistic works.

I can truly say, that because of this couple's deep and close relationship with God, they were divinely equipped with the virtues of compassion and love for the poor. Roman and Margaret had used their time, talent and resources to help the disadvantaged to live a quality and better life mainly through education.

A philanthropic person deeply involves himself in a worthy cause, not just for charitable donations, but for the improvement of human welfare and dignity. As philanthropists, Margaret and Roman had firmly believed that education is the key to a person's success and the magic way to get a good job in order to live a decent and comfortable lifestyle. Their inability to have children of their own, wasn't a deterrent at all from achieving their mission, but rather had served more as a catalyst to passionately execute their absolute love and utmost care for the poor through their acts of great community service. So, they both wholeheartedly dedicated their entire life in service to the poor children's education, thus had fostered tremendous number of recipients, whose lives had improved for the better.

Roman and Margaret were God's messengers to make this world a better place to live in. They had also, devotedly taught people to have faith and trust in the Lord as they moved on in their life journey.

Marco, as one of the beneficiaries, as well as his daughter, had shared this strikingly-outstanding philanthropic power couple worthy of emulation! Thank you, Lord God for their great love to mankind, through YOU and the power of the Most Holy Spirit! Praise God! Amen!

"Serve one another with the gifts each of you received, thus, becoming good managers of the varied graces of God. If you speak, deliver the word of God; if you have a special ministry, let it be seen as God's power so that in everything God may be glorified in Jesus Christ. To Him belong glory and power forever and ever. Amen."
(1 Peter 4: 10-11)

Conclusion

Did you enjoy the life journey of each story? Have you found out why I called them as "Treasured Stories inspired by the Holy Spirit? Which story had touched and moved you most? Why?

Personally, I loved and cherished all of these stories. Each amazing story had its own uniqueness, but all of them had definitely displayed the powerful inspiration from the Holy Spirit. Each character came from different walks of life, yet all of them had used the same inspiration and power from the Holy Spirit! The characters' strong faith and trust in the Lord were all manifested in their life journey. All of them had struggled in life, and in the end, had triumphantly reaped the glorious rewards from God's love and generosity.

Man's weakness towards temptation had been in existence since creation – the time of Adam and Eve. This weakness still lingers around and attacks the most vulnerable, the people who are in the midst of trials, persecution and challenges. At this point, if man had lost his connection with God, he becomes the best object to be trapped towards the pit of darkness. That's why during man's period of pains and sufferings, it is crucial to hold on towards God's grace and mercy, in order to be saved from the onslaught of the evil. This is the most critical period where man seeks inspiration, enlightenment and guidance from the power of the Holy Spirit.

As revealed from the treasured stories in this book, the characters had experienced different trials in their journey. Some fell deeply into the trap of evil; some absolutely committed big mistakes in their decisions; others were totally derailed into the right path, but all of them, in the end stood up and firmly held their heads up towards heaven and gladly received the inspiration and power of the Most Holy Spirit and had straightened up their crooked ways through God's guidance. Thus, I'd noted these life journeys as Treasured Stories inspired by the Holy Spirit, because they are like gems of different stones, colours and shapes, but they have all the same extraordinary beauty, once they had wholeheartedly succumbed into the light and power of the Holy Spirit. This book was precisely written to share these treasures to people for motivation and inspiration in their everyday encounters and challenges in life.

I have to repeat one of my favourite quotations which I'd learned from my German nun friend, which states: "A beautiful life does not just happen. It is built daily by prayers, humility, sacrifice and love." The deep meaning of this quotation is evidently proven true, through the inspirational stories I had included in this book. The quotation itself explains and displays the clear picture of why and how the characters victoriously had achieved their glorious and beautiful life, mainly from the inspiration of the Holy Spirit!

Allow me to give you this acronym **'H O L Y'** and firmly entreat you to reflect its importance.

H – Holiness – God has planned His people who are created in His own image and likeness, to be holy as He is holy, as written in 1 Peter 1:16, "Since scriptures says: Be holy, for I am holy." I know that it's not easy, but we can pray and ask Jesus to bless our soul, to be thirsty more for holiness than worldliness and make us holy in every aspect of our character, actions and decisions. Growing in holiness is a process in the presence of the Holy Spirit's guidance to overcome temptations and more focused to the image of Christ.

O – Obedience – God wants His people to be obedient to His plan. It is hearing God's word and acting on it. It is following His will for us; it is doing what God has asked us to do, and totally surrendering under His authority. Again, we desperately need the presence of the Holy Spirit in our life in order to clearly identify and know the plan and will of God for us and act on our submissive compliance under His authority.

L - Love – God is love. Whoever lives in love, lives in God, and God in him. God clearly gave us His commandments on how to love and be His disciple as written in John 13:34-35, "A new commandment I give you, love one another. Just as I have loved you, you also must love one another. By this everyone will know that you are my disciples, if you have love for one another."

Y – Yes – Yes, to God's plan and will to us! We aim to constantly have an affirmative response whenever an opportunity arises to be closer to God like being His true disciple and follower like some of these biblical characters who said Yes to God's call to action: Noah to build the ark, Moses to lead his people, Esther to save her people, Mary to give birth to the Messiah, Joseph to be the foster father of Jesus, and many more. Throughout the Bible we find many people who trusted God and said "Yes Lord" to His will for their lives. As a true disciple of Jesus, we pray to be holy, obedient and loving and boldly and fearless say "YES LORD, here I am! Send me."

It is my sincerest hope that you've found enjoyment and took some good 'take-aways' from these inspirational stories, which hopefully would help you in your own journey!

Rest assured that you are in my prayers and please include me too in your prayers. See you again in the next book I will be writing as the Holy Spirit leads me. God bless you!

Lanni Fides
September 29, 2022

ABOUT THE AUTHOR

Lanni Fides is a former high school teacher and college professor who migrated from the Philippines to Australia with her family in 1988. In 1991, the family joined Couples for Christ, NSW Australia, became a couple-leader of a mission team in the northern region of the country, and a coordinator of NSW Handmaids of the Lord, a ministry for women of the community. Currently, she is still an active member of the seniors' group in her local community.

As a retiree, she's an active servant of St. John 23rd Parish, Stanhope Gardens, NSW, and a catechist of the same schools of the parish under the Ministry of Special Religious Education of the Diocese.

Her main mission in writing books is to proclaim God's unconditional love and faithfulness to His people. Her first book entitled: Encounters with God through Dreams and Visions was published on April 11, 2022. Shortly after, her second book entitled: 46 Years After … "The Sign" was released on July 7, 2022.

"May God, the source of hope, fill you with joy and peace in your faith, so that your hope may increase greatly by the power of the Holy Spirit." (Romans 15:13)

"If we live in the Spirit, let us also walk in the Spirit." (Galatians 5:25)

Lanni Fides
09.29.22

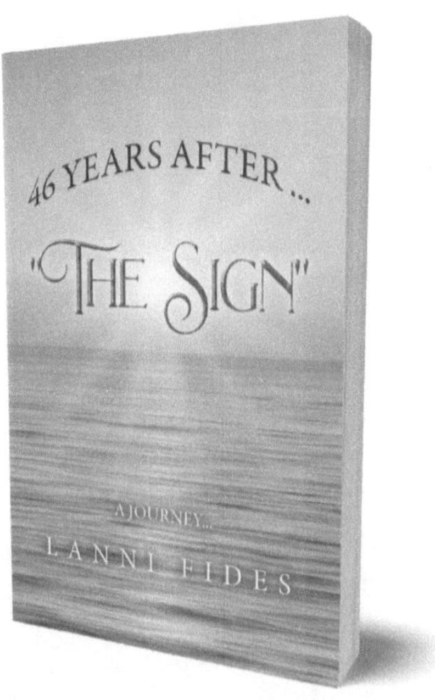

Have you ever experienced being caught at a crossroads, confused which road to follow?

This is the stage in one's life where an important decision has to be made. Have you asked God's guidance and wisdom? All the time, I had! To be a nun or a married woman was my crossroads. Family mission impelled me to be a married woman, but I needed a sign from heaven for the right man! This testimonial book unfolds the significant decision I'd made immediately after the Sign was prompted to me through the Holy Spirit! It is a journey on my 46 years of marriage and a family-life memoir showcasing God's presence in our family. Do you want to know what the Sign is all about and its impact on our lives? Then take time to read this book, with the hope of keeping some precious take-aways. Enjoy the journey with God!

---

amazon.com

chapters.indigo.ca

barnesandnoble.com

booktopia.com.au